**Mediaeval Sources in Translation 41**

Raymond of Penyafort

SUMMA ON MARRIAGE

# Saint Michael's College
# Mediaeval Translations

*Editorial Committee*

Joseph Goering
Giulio Silano

# Raymond of Penyafort

# Summa on Marriage

Translated with an Introduction by

Pierre J. Payer

Pontifical Institute of Mediaeval Studies

This book has been published with the help of a grant from the
Canadian Federation for the Humanities and Social Sciences,
through the Aid to Scholarly Publications Programme,
using funds provided by the
Social Sciences and Humanities Research Council of Canada.

LIBRARY AND ARCHIVES CANADA CATALOGUING IN PUBLICATION

Raymond, of Peñafort, Saint, 1175?-1275
    Summa on marriage / Raymond of Penyafort ; translated with an
introduction by Pierre J. Payer.

(Mediaeval sources in translation ; 41)
Includes bibliographical references and index.
ISBN 0-88844-291-2

    1. Marriage (Canon Law).    2. Marriage–History–To 1500–Sources.
I. Payer, Pierre J., 1936-.    II. Pontifical Institute of Mediaeval Studies.
III. Title.    IV. Series.

BX2250.R39 2005                    262.9'33                    C2005-902035-0

© 2005 by

Pontifical Institute of Mediaeval Studies
59 Queen's Park Crescent East
Toronto, Ontario, Canada M5S 2C4

www.pims.ca

Printed in Canada

# Contents

# Abbreviations

*Auth.*      *Authenticum,* a medieval collection of laws drawn from Justinian's *Novels.* For ease of reference, citations will be to the modern edition of Justinian's *Novels* rather than to the medieval collection.

*Code*       Justinian, *Codex Justinianus,* ed. Paul Krueger, Corpus iuris civilis, vol. 2 (Berlin, 1959).

*Compil.*    *Quinque compilationes antiquae,* ed. Aemilius Friedberg (Leipzig, 1882; reprint Graz, 1956).

*Dig.*       *The Digest of Justinian,* Latin Text, ed. T. Mommsen and Paul Krueger, English translation edited by Alan Watson, 4 vols. (Philadelphia, 1985).

*Decretum*   *Corpus iuris canonici. Pars prior. Decretum magistri Gratiani,* ed. Aemilius Friedberg (Leipzig, 1879; reprint Graz, 1959).

*Inst.*      *Justinian's Institutes,* translated with an introduction by Peter Birks and Grant McLeod with the Latin text of Paul Krueger (Ithaca, N.Y., 1987).

*Novels*     Justinian, *Novellae,* ed. R. Schoell and W. Kroll, Corpus iuris civilis, vol. 3 (Berlin, 1959).

*Sent.*      Peter Lombard, *Sententiae in IV libris distinctae,* Tomus II (Liber III et IV), Spicilegium Bonaventurianum, 5 (Rome, 1981).

X            Gregory IX, *Decretalium collectiones. Corpus iuris canonici. Pars secunda. Decretalium collectiones,* ed. Aemilius Friedberg (Leipzig, 1879; reprint Graz, 1959).

# Introduction

Raymond of Penyafort (ca. 1180-1275) was born in Catalonia in the vicinity of Barcelona where he studied and later taught the basic arts course in the cathedral school. He went on to study and teach law at the famous centre of Bologna (see below, Title 25, introd.). Shortly after returning to Barcelona Raymond entered the Dominican order (ca. 1223).

Raymond's subsequent life might best be characterized as one of service – service to his order and service to the Church. On entering the Dominican order Raymond wrote a summary account of penance to help his Dominican confreres and others in resolving doubts and unravelling knotty questions that might arise in hearing confessions.[1] This was by far the most significant and influential practical work on penance and confession until the end of the century. Then John of Freiburg, O.P. made over Raymond's summa, wedding Raymond and Thomas Aquinas into a juridico-theological synthesis that set the style for such works for centuries.[2]

In 1230 Raymond was called to the papal court of Gregory IX (1227-1241) as confessor and papal penitentiary. However, his great service was in acceding to Gregory's request to compile a collection of law out of Gregory's own constitutions and decretals and those of his predecessors.[3] This was a significant, officially sanctioned collection of ecclesiastical law. Raymond seems to have completed the task in 1234 and Gregory IX promulgated the collection (known today as the *Decretals of Gregory IX*) on 5 September 1234, acknowledging his "dear son, brother Raymond."[4]

---

[1] Raymond of Penyafort, *Summa de paenitentia*, edited by X. Ochoa and A. Díez, Universa bibliotheca iuris, vol. 1, tomus B (Rome, 1976) col. 277. See M. Michèle Mulchahey, *"First the Bow Is Bent in Study . . ." Dominican Education before 1350*, Studies and Texts, 132 (Toronto, 1998) pp. 533-539.

[2] See A. Walz, "Si. Raymundi de Penyafort auctoritas in re poenitentiali," *Angelicum* 12 (1935): 346-396 (pp. 373-396 re influence); Leonard E. Boyle, "The *Summa confessorum* of John of Freiburg and the Popularization of the Moral Teaching of St. Thomas and of Some of His Contemporaries," in *St. Thomas Aquinas, 1274-1974. Commemorative Studies*, ed. A. Maurer, et al. (Toronto, 1974) vol. 2, pp. 245-268.

[3] See S. Kuttner, "Raymond of Peñafort as editor. The 'decretals' and 'constitutions' of Gregory IX," *Bulletin of Medieval Canon Law*, n.s. 12 (1982): 65-80.

[4] Gregory IX, Letter "Rex pacificus," in X (col. 2-4).

Shortly after leaving the papal household Raymond reluctantly accepted election to be Master General of his order. He provided an important service to the Dominicans in revising their constitutions and when completed he resigned after just two years (1240). On returning to Spain Raymond seems to have spent the rest of his life in the missionary service of the Church to the Moors and the Jews. To advance this work he encouraged the Dominicans to establish linguistic schools in Arabic and Hebrew.[5] In the same spirit he had Thomas Aquinas compose the *Summa contra Gentiles*, a presentation of the rational grounds of the Christian faith.[6]

Curiously, Raymond did not include a treatment of marriage in his early account of penance. "Curiously" because numerous issues touching on marriage would certainly arise in the confessions of ordinary Christians, e.g., conditions for legitimate engagements and marriages, the intricate types of prohibited relationships of consanguinity and affinity, and proper and improper marital sexual relations. It is generally believed by contemporary scholars that for marriage questions Raymond assumed his readers would have had recourse to a popular work on marriage by the canonist Tancred. In fact, Tancred's *Summa de matrimonio* was appended to Raymond's work in several manuscripts, perhaps added by Raymond himself.[7] Both Raymond and Tancred grounded themselves largely on Gratian's *Decretum* (ca. 1140) and various collections of ecclesiastical law compiled after Gratian.[8]

Raymond took advantage of his own labours on the *Decretals* to update his earlier summa on penance. Further, with the fourth book of the *Decretals* providing a contemporary collection of law on marriage, Tancred's work was no longer adequate. Consequently, at the same time Raymond composed a summa on marriage that can, not incorrectly, be seen as a complete revision and updating of Tancred's *Summa de matrimonio*.[9] By 1241 the second edition of

[5] See Mulchahey, *"First the Bow Is Bent in Study ..."*, pp. 344-348.

[6] For orientation to biographical and bibliographical material see Giulio Silano, "Raymond of Peñafort, S.," *Dictionary of the Middle Ages* 10, pp. 266-267; P. Stenger, "Raymond of Peñafort, St.," *New Catholic Encyclopedia* 12, p. 105.

[7] See Raymond of Penyafort, *Summa de matrimonio*, edited by X. Ochoa and A. Díez, Universa bibliotheca iuris, vol. 1, tomus C (Rome, 1978) Prolegomena, pp. CXX-CXXXI; Tancred, *Summa de matrimonio*, ed. Agathon Wunderlich (Göttingen, 1841); L. Chevallier, "Tancredus," *DDC* 7 (1965): 1146-1165;

[8] See, *Quinque Compilationes antiquae nec non Collectio canonum Lipsiensis*, ed. Aemilius Friedberg (Leipzig, 1882; reprint Graz, 1956).

[9] See Raymond of Penyafort, *Summa de matrimonio*, Prolegomena, pp. CXX-CXXII (relation to Tancred). Raymond's editors are at pains to counter the view that he plagiarized Tancred (ibid., pp. CXXII-CXXIV). Of course, an accusation of plagiarism is anacronistic. However, a parallel reading of Tancred and Raymond cannot avoid being struck by Raymond's adherence to Tancred's material, order, titles, wording, references, and Raymond did not even see fit to alter Tancred's personal conclusion. Kuttner's claim that Raymond's *Summa de matrimonio* is

Raymond's work on penance and his account of marriage where adorned with an insightful and helpful gloss by William of Rennes, O.P.[10] Raymond's accounts of penance and marriage played a significant role in the education of future Dominican priests and provided an important resource for the exercise of their pastoral ministry. I suspect the remark of one Dominican author of an instructional manual for those destined for the pastoral ministry is representative of a general attitude. When Simon of Hinton deals with marriage in his *Ad instructionem iuniorum* (1260 x 1262) he says that he does not have to say a great deal about it because Raymond deals with it sufficiently. Clearly, the assumption is that Raymond's account would be available for consultation and so there would be no need to repeat it.[11]

The 1603 edition of Raymond presents his composition as one work, with the treatment of marriage constituting its fourth book. Such a conception is not unusual, being reflected in manuscripts and in early editions. However, does it reflect Raymond's conception? His recent editors are insistent that the treatment of marriage was not conceived of as a fourth book of the summa on penance, but as a separate composition. Contemporary scholars seem to accept this view and it is suggested by Raymond's own words, "after the small summa on penance I have offered to the honour of God and the progress of souls a special treatise on marriage."[12] Besides, Raymond did seem to conceive of his work as a revision of Tancred's work, which was an independent composition.

If that is the case, what ought the title of this separate composition to be? This is a notoriously difficult question to answer for many medieval works whose manuscripts were often graced with different titles by different copyists. The editors list fifteen titles in alphabetical order with references to at least one

---

simply a reworking of Tancred is a fair judgment [S. Kuttner, *Repertorium der Kanonistik (1140-1234). Prodomus corporis glossarum*, t. 1, Studi e testi, 71 (Vatican City, 1937) p. 445]. The principal reworking was Raymond's replacing the decretal references to the compilations created after Gratian with references to the same decretals as they appear in the *Decretals* of Gregory IX. A refined analysis of Raymond's originality would require a superior edition of Tancred. See Amédée Teetaert, "Summa de matrimonio de Saint Raymund de Penyafort," *Jus pontificium* 9 (1929): 54-61, 228-234, 312-322.

[10] See Mulchahey, "*First the Bow Is Bent in Study* ...," p. 542; R. Naz, "Guillaume de Rennes," *DDC* 5, col. 1080. The gloss was added to numerous manuscripts of Raymond and accompanied the printed editions of his work.

[11] Simon of Hinton, *Ad instructionem iuniorum*, among the works of Jean Gerson, *Compendium theologiae breve et utile*, Opera omnia (Antwerp, 1706) vol. 1, col. 290-291. See Jean Gerson, *Oeuvres complètes. 1. Introduction générale*, ed. P. Glorieux (Paris, 1960) p. 41; A. Dondaine, "La Somme de Simon de Hinton," *RTAM* 9 (1937): 5-22, 205-218.

[12] Below, Preface. See *Summa Sti. Raymundi de Peniafort Barcinonensis Ord. Praedicator. De poenitentia et matrimonio cum glossis Ioannis de Friburgo* [i.e., the gloss of William of Rennes, not John of Freiburg] (Rome, 1603; rpt. Gregg, 1967); Raymond of Penyafort, *Summa de matrimonio*, Prolegomena, pp. CXV-CXVIII.

manuscript for each usage. Their conclusion is that "the true title of the work seems to be *Summa de matrimonio*."[13] Most of the manuscripts use this title and Raymond himself refers to the work under that title. Again, it might be expected that if Raymond was providing a revision of Tancred, he would use Tancred's title.

As he notes in his preface Raymond's goal was to help resolve doubts and confusions about marriage that often arise in the context of penance and confession.[14] He says he will deal with three areas, but a more refined analysis can detect six broad topics:

1. Engagements (title 1)
2. Marriage (title 2)
3. Impediments to marriage (titles 3-18)
4. Legal procedure in marriage cases (titles 19-23)
5. The legitimacy of children (title 24)
6. Dowries and gifts in view of marriage (title 25).

By the time of Raymond's writing marriage was well under ecclesiastical jurisdiction both as to the determination of the conditions for a valid marriage as well as to the legal procedures devised to deal with issues arising from the application of those conditions. From this point of view marriage must be conceived of as a legal entity governed by an intricate set of rules and regulations. Of course marriage was much more, involving love, affection, respect, the raising of children to the honour of God. However, these desirable features had to rest on the firm foundation of a valid marriage, which was determined by ecclesiastical law.[15] I have been speaking of ecclesiastical laws, but it should be noted that while all of these laws received ecclesiastical expression they were not all of purely ecclesiastical origin. Raymond notes this on several occasions. For example, he introduces his treatment of the impediment of error about a person in this manner, "First, the impediment of error about a person. Unlike several impediments, it excludes consent by its very nature, not through the regulation of the Church ..." (T. 3.1).

These laws were to be found in the collectiion of Gratian (ca. 1140) and collections of constitutions and papal letters after Gratian up to pope Hon-

---

[13] Raymond of Penyafort, *Summa de matrimonio*, Prolegomena, p. CXIX.

[14] I suspect the work would be beyond the financial and intellectual resources of most ordinary parish priests. It would be more useful and accessible to the higher clergy (e.g., bishops, archdeacons, deans) and to academics (the use of Raymond in Dominican schools). It would, in the language of Innocent III and Honorius III in the introduction to the third and fifth compilations, be useful "both in [making] judgments and in the schools" ("tam in iudiciis quam in scholis"). *Quinque compilationes antiquae*, pp. 105, 151.

[15] For an excellent summary see Michael M. Sheehan, "Family and Marriage, Western European," *Dictionary of the Middle Ages* 4, pp. 608-612. For the early thirteenth century see James A. Brundage, *Law, Sex, and Christian Society in Medieval Europe* (Chicago, 1987) pp. 325-80, 405-16.

orius III (1216-1227). The latter were gathered over time into five principal collections known as the *Quinque compilations antiquae* (*Five Ancient Compilations*).[16] Raymond, at the behest of pope Gregory IX, brought this process to a close with his compilations of the *Decretals of Gregory IX*, incorporating much from the five previous compilations, from Gregory, and from other material deemed relevant by Raymond.

Raymond's *Summa on Marriage*, building on Tancred and drawing on his own work on the decretals, presents a fine summary of the current law on marriage. The first three quarters of the work focuses on the central requirements for valid engagements (Title 1) and marriage (T. 2). Free consent was central to this medieval view of marriage. Seven was considered the minimum age required for the promise of future marriage (engagements). Even if an earlier engagement was made by parents, it had to be ratified in some clear way by the party involved on reaching the age for engagements. Following an ancient tradition age differentiation was required for marriage – twelve for girls, fourteen for boys. In his discussion of marriage Raymond diverges from his mainly legal approach to discuss the goods of marriage and how they are said to excuse marital sexual relations (T. 2.12-13).

About half of Raymond's summa deals with the diriment impediments to marriage, that is, the basic conditions whose presence invalidates marriage and dissolves those already undertaken. These impediments focus principally on three areas. First, that of freedom of consent, which is undermined by force (T. 11) or by an error in regard to the identity of the person one chooses to marry (T. 3). A second impediment was called impotence by Raymond, the impossibility of engaging in sexual intercourse (T. 16), as a pre-existing condition before the marriage. Given the centrality of procreation to the purpose of marriage, clearly impotence would undermine this very possibility. Finally, the third area embraced the whole range of relationships that determined eligibility for marriage: blood relationships (T. 6), relationships through marriage (T. 15), spiritual relationships arising from baptism or confirmation (T. 7), legal relations through adoption (T. 8). The work concludes with legal refinements on the separation or reunion of marriages (T. 19-22), the identification of legitimate and illegitimate children (T. 24), and dowries (T. 25).

Raymond's *Summa on Marriage* faithfully captures the core idea of marriage as a divine institution (T.2.5-6), whose realization in the world was governed by ecclesiastical laws. The work translated below presents the author's marshalling and interpretation of those laws and provides constant reference to the legal sources on which the teaching depends. He did not make the law, he presented and interpreted it. The *Summa on Marriage* offers contemporary

[16] See Brundage, *Law, Sex, and Christian Society*, pp. 326-327.

readers a reliable picture of the basic medieval conception of marriage and the conditions required for its validity. For readers who do not read Latin, this translation is the only such work available in English.

An appendix and two indexes have been added to the translation. The appendix presents parallels between Raymond's treatment in his *Summa on Marriage* and Thomas Aquinas' treatment of marriage in his early commentary on the *Sentences* of Peter Lombard. Particularly on the subject of marriage one encounters in Aquinas a balanced synthesis of theology, Aristotelian philosophy, and ecclesiastical law. Raymond of Penyafort seems to have been a source for some of the ecclesiastical law. The appendix does not claim unreservedly that Aquinas used Raymond, but I believe the parallels between the two authors are sufficiently striking to justify presenting them in tabular form. In some cases the parallels perhaps reflect no more than a common tradition shared by canonists and theologians alike, e.g., the definitions of consanguinity, affinity, spiritual relationship, and the mnemonic verses associated with those subjects. In other cases the parallels suggest a use of Raymond by Aquinas, e.g., the four ways of contracting engagements (T. 1.1), the seven cases in which an adulteress wife cannot be dismissed by her husband (T. 22.3). It will be noted that this appendix also provides references to the Supplement of Aquinas' *Summa of Theology*. After his death the Supplement was made up of passages from Aquinas' commentary on the *Sentences* of Peter Lombard in an effort to compensate for the unfinished *Summa of Theology*. Since the Supplement has been published as part of the *Summa of Theology*, it has been translated into English.

The "Index of Legal References" provides an overview of Raymond's use of both ecclesiastical and Roman law. This index can be used in conjunction with Professor Brundage's "Index of Legal Sources" to compare Raymond's use and interpretation with other medieval writers cited by Brundage.[17]

With few exceptions references in the translation are to Roman law and to Gratian and the *Decretals of Gregory IX*. Roman law has been well served by translators (see list of abbreviations). Unfortunately, the same cannot be said for ecclesiastical or canon law. References to the latter are made to the standard edition by Friedberg (see list of abbreviations).[18]

[17] Brundage, *Law, Sex, and Christian Society*, pp. 663-674.

[18] The legal exceptions are to the older *Compilationes antiquae* in Title 10 (*Quinque Compilationes antiquae nec non Collectio canonum Lipsiensis*, ed. Aemilius Friedberg [Leipzig, 1882; reprint Graz, 1956]) and to the canonist Huguccio, *Summa decretorum* in Title 10.6 and Title 14.2. For Huguccio I used the manuscript, Admont, Stiftsbibliothek 7, fols. 2ra-500rb; see A. M. Stickler, "Uguccio de Pise," *DDC* 7 (1965) cols. 1355-1362; Kenneth Pennington, "Huguccio," *Dictionary of the Middle Ages*, 6, pp. 327-328.

## Note on the Edition

The reader who wishes to consult Raymond's *summa* in the original Latin has two main alternatives, each with its own merits and limitations. The *editio princeps* was printed in Rome in 1603 under the title *Summa Sancti Raymundi de Peniafort, Barcinonensis, Ordinis praedicator, De poenitentia et matrimonio, cum glossis Ioannis de Friburgo*. The text, accompanied by the mid-thirteenth-century commentry of William of Rennes (and not John of Freiburg as stated on the title page), has served as the basis for the study of Raymond's work ever since. It was conveniently reprinted by Gregg Press (Farnborough, UK) in 1967.

In 1978 a new edition was produced by X. Ochoa and A. Díez.[19] Several criticisms have been levelled at this edition (as well as editions of other works by Raymond of Penyafort in the series): (1) failure to provide an adequate critical edition based on a consideration of all the manuscripts, their interrelations, and transmission;[20] (2) a not entirely faithful rendering even of the few manuscripts used;[21] (3) the practice of relegating Raymond's supporting references to footnotes.[22]

These criticisms are appropriate, and readers of the Latin text and the translation ought to be aware of them. The first criticism cannot be gainsaid, although one might question the practicality of providing a traditional critical edition of a work represented by hundreds of manuscripts. The second criticism is a function of the skill and care of the editors. Ordinary readers have no way of assessing such skill and care unless they have the relevant manuscripts to hand. One must assume the adequacy of the transcriptions of edited texts.[23] Thorough technical reviews will either justify the assumption or provide cautions about the adequacy of the transcription.

The third criticism is also well-taken. The thirteenth century had no system of footnoting so authors ran their supporting references in the body of the text. To relegate these references to numbered footnotes in an edition of the Latin text does do a disservice to the edition and does not properly reflect Raymond's methodology. However, I believe things are otherwise for an English translation. In this case, to leave Raymond's references in the body of the text

---

[19] Raymond of Penyafort, *Summa de matrimonio*, edited by X. Ochoa and A. Díez, Universa bibliotheca iuris, vol. 1, tomus C (Rome, 1978).

[20] See Stephan Kuttner, "On the Method of Editing Medieval Authors," *The Jurist* 37 (1977): 385-386. This is a general comment on the series Universa bibliotheca iuris.

[21] See James A. Brundage's review, *The Jurist* 39 (1979): 516. Brundage does not address the *Summa de matrimonio* but pays "special attention" (p. 514) to the *Summa de paenitentia* by way of illustrating his critique of both editions.

[22] Kuttner, "On the Method of Editing Medieval Authors," p. 385.

[23] Brundage review, *The Jurist* 39 (1979): 516.

would be far too distracting to the modern English reader, who is probably more interested in the content of Raymond's argument than in the supporting documentation. For that reason Raymond's sources have been moved to numbered footnotes (marked by "RdeP"). Those who are interested in the sources can easily find them by consulting the notes. Raymond used standard medieval abbreviations in his references ("Extra" and "ff"), which are reproduced in the notes; these references are followed by their modern forms in square brackets. The footnotes to the translation also incorporate modern comments by the translator and others, also in square brackets.

Raymond of Penyafort, O.P.

Summa on Marriage

# [Preface]

Since doubts, yes sometimes even apparent confusions about marriage frequently arise in the penitential forum, after the small summa on penance[1] I have offered to the honour of God and for the progress of souls a special treatise on marriage. It discusses in an orderly way first engagements and marriage, second the fifteen impediments to marriage,[2] third how one deals with preserving or dissolving a marriage, children (particularly legitimate children), and dowries and marriage gifts. I have inserted titles in appropriate places and diverse doubtful matters relevant to the individual titles.

## [INDEX OF TITLES]

---

[1] [This is a reference to Raymond's own, *Summa de paenitentia*, edited by X. Ochoa and A. Díez, Universa bibliotheca iuris, vol. 1, tome B (Rome, 1976). I take Raymond's reference to be to the work in general and not to its title.]

[2] [See below Title 1.16 where Raymond notes there are fourteen impediments (12 that both impede a marriage from being contracted and break off one already contracted, and two that impede a marriage from being contracted but do not break off one already contracted). See Bernard of Pavia (ca. 1198), who says there are fourteen impediments, *Summa de matrimonio III*, in *Faventini episcopi Summa Decretalium*, edited by E. A. T. Laspeyres (Regensberg, 1860; Graz, 1956) p. 287. See Tancred (1210 x 1214), *Summa de matrimonio*, edited by Agathon Wunderlich (Göttingen, 1841) Title 15 (p. 17).]

# Title I
## Engagements

Engagements must be dealt with first since engagements customarily precede marriage. So we must look at: what engagements are; the etymology of the word; how they are contracted; at what age they can be contracted; the effect of engagements; whether engagements can be broken.

1.    An engagement is a promise of future marriage.[1] The term "sponsalia" (engagement) is from "spondendo" (pledging), that is, promising.

Engagements are contracted in four ways: sometimes by a mere promise; sometimes by giving an engagement pledge; sometimes with the addition of an engagement ring; sometimes with the addition of an oath.

By a mere promise, when a man says, "I will take you as my wife," and the woman replies, "I will take you as my husband," or equivalent words. When they are contracted in that way through words in the future tense, they are true engagements. But if they are contracted through words in the present tense, because the man says "I take you as my wife" and she "I take you as my husband" or they use similar words that signify the mutual consent of both in the present tense, for example when he says, "I consent to you as to my wife" and she says the same, or "From this time I will hold on to and have you for my wife, and I will keep faith with you as my wife," and the wife in turn speaks similarly to the man, these are called engagements about the present, but improperly. It is truly a marriage, so that, even though he does not know her carnally, neither is allowed to marry another, and if he should, even if he knows the second carnally, he must be separated from her and be compelled to return to the first.[2]

Again, they are contracted by giving an engagement pledge such as money or other things.[3]

The pledge of an engagement ring, which is popularly called an engagement but is properly called a pledge, is dealt with in [Gratian].[4]

---

[1] RdeP: 30 q. 5 "Nostrates" [*Decretum* C. 30 q.5 c.3]; ff. *de sponsalibus*, Lex 1 [*Dig.* 23.1.1].

[2] RdeP: Extra *de sponsalibus*, "Ex parte E. mulieris" [X 4.1.9], "Si inter virum" [X 4.1.31]; *de sponsa duorum*, c. 1 et c. ult. [X 4.4.1 and 5].

[3] RdeP: C. *de sponsalibus*, Lex "Arris" [*Code* 5.1.3].

[4] RdeP: 27 q. 2 "Si quis desponsaverit" [*Decretum* C. 27 q.2 c.15].

The oath is dealt with at Extra *de sponsalibus,* "De illis,"[5] "Praeterea."[6]

2.   An examination of the age at which engagements can be contracted follows. They can be contracted after the seventh year because then both boys and girls are said to have discretion, and engagements are usually attractive to them then.[7]

But if they or their parents in their name contract an engagement before the seventh year, they accomplish nothing.[8] Even though they are contracted before age seven or in the cradle, if, when they reach the age of seven, they begin to find the engagement attractive, it takes effect from that time, so that even if the espoused male does not know her carnally, he cannot have her blood relative as a wife, or vice versa.[9]

Otherwise, the appropriate age for a girl to contract marriage is twelve, for a boy it is fourteen.[10] And if they are united beforehand, there is no marriage.

3.   Some questions can be raised here. Suppose a pre-pubescent boy and girl contract marriage with words in the present tense. The question is whether there is any effect, for it seems that marriage was not contracted because of the age impediment, nor engagement because the form of the words is not suited to engagement but to marriage.

For this I make a distinction: either they only intend to contract marriage with these words and not an engagement, or they intend simply to contract what they can, as if they said, "If what I am doing has no effect in the sense I am doing it, let it have the effect that it can." In the first case there is no effect — no marriage because they are unable to marry, no engagement because that is not their intent. In the second case, however, an engagement in reference to the future stands. These texts can be understood in this way.[11]

4.   Suppose that children before age seven contract an engagement or a marriage through words in the present tense; or after age seven before puberty they are joined matrimonially through words in the present tense. In the case of the first children, are engagements confirmed by such an act after age seven? Or in the case of the others is marriage confirmed with the onset of puberty?

---

[5] [X 4.1.5].

[6] [X 4.1.12].

[7] RdeP: Extra *de desponsatione impuberum,* "Litteras" [X 4.2.4].

[8] RdeP: 30 q. 2 "Ubi non est consensus" [*Decretum* C. 30 q.2 c.1].

[9] RdeP: Extra *de desponsatione impuberum,* "Litteras" [X 4.2.4], "Accessit" [X 4.2.5], "Duo pueri" [X 4.2.12].

[10] RdeP: Extra *de desponsatione impuberum,* "Puberes" [X 4.2.3], "Continebatur" [X 4.2. 6].

[11] RdeP: Extra *de desponsatione impuberum,* "Tuae nobis" [X 4.2.14]; et arg. Extra *eodem titulo,* "Duo pueri" [X 4.2.12], et Extra *de conditionibus appositis,* "Super eo" [X 4.5.5].

To this you should say that if, on reaching the legal age, they understand what was done and expressly consider it valid or even tacitly (which is presumed from the sole fact that they do not contradict it) the engagement or marriage seems to be ratified, particularly if they were residing together.[12] Again, and on the basis of the same laws, I believe [the same] if the parents contracted the engagement or marriage for their children, or in the name of the children.[13]

5. Suppose an adult male contracts through words in the present tense with a minor girl, who, however, is close to marriageable age, or vice versa; or suppose two who are pre-pubescent but close to puberty contract. Does the marriage stand?

Say that if prudence supplies for age and they have joined carnally by mutual consent, or if from the bodily development they exhibit it appears they are capable of carnal union, the marriage stands.[14] I said "by mutual consent" because if there was intercourse through violence and the girl was unwilling, she would not seem to prejudice herself thereby.[15]

It also seems they should not be more than six months from puberty, even though the other things I spoke of above are present.[16] Several teachers say this unconditionally[17] and I believe it is true, unless they joined carnally with common consent. Then I believe it safer to judge in favour of the marriage, even if they were more than six months from the legal age.[18]

## THE EFFECT OF ENGAGEMENTS

6. Next the effect of engagements is examined. Note that engagements are contracted sometimes conditionally, sometimes unconditionally.[19] See below [Title 4.3] for what must be held on this matter.[20]

---

[12] RdeP: Extra *De desponsatione impuberum*, "Litteras" [X 4.2.4], "Accessit" [X 4.2.5], "Duo pueri" [X 4.2.12]; Extra *de conditionibus appositis*, "Super eo" [X 4.5.5].

[13] RdeP: These are relevant: 32 q. 2 "Non omnis" [*Decretum* C. 32 q.2 c.12], et § "Cum ergo" [*Decretum* C. 32 q.2 d.p.c.12].

[14] RdeP: Extra *de desponsatione impuberum*, "Puberes" [X 4.2.3], "Continebatur" [X 4.2.6], "A nobis" [X 4.2.8], "De illis" (secundo) [X 4.2.9], "Attestationes" [X 4.2.10], "Ex litteris" [X 4.2.11]; Extra *de sponsalibus*, c. ult. [X 4.1.32].

[15] RdeP: As in "Continebatur" [X 4.2.6]; 32 q. 5 "Proposito" [*Decretum* C. 32 q.5 c.4], "Ad Dominum" [*Decretum* C. 32 q.5 c.7].

[16] RdeP: Arg. Extra *de desponsatione impuberum*, "Continebatur" [X 4.2.6], "Tuae" [X 4.2.14]; ff. *de excusationibus tutorum*, "Non tamen" [*Dig.* 27.1.17].

[17] Text: *simpliciter*

[18] RdeP: Extra *de desponsatione impuberum*, "A nobis" [X 4.2.8], "De illis" [X 4.2.9].

[19] Text: *pure*.

[20] RdeP: *De impedimento conditionis*, § "Circa conditiones" [p. 34].

In sum, it must not be overlooked that although engagements can be contracted under the condition that a promised sum of money will be paid, as was said, nonetheless money cannot be promised as a matter of penalty. If it were, the promise of a penalty does not stand nor can it be sought; for example, if it were said, "If I do not contract with you, I will give you a hundred marks," since the addition of the penalty has no weight because marriages ought to be free.[21]

If engagements are unconditionally[22] contracted, either both are of majority age, that is, adults, or both minors below age twelve or fourteen and over seven, or one is of majority age and the other a minor. In such cases the engagements stand, since, if they do not because they were not seven years old, they can seek release before the time of puberty.[23]

If both are of majority of age and they added oaths and afterwards one wishes to withdraw, disregarding the many varied opinions that have been written on the matter and saving a better judgment, I believe that if it can be presumed with probability that through a sentence of excommunication he would be induced to keep the oath, or perhaps war or serious scandal is feared unless the oath is kept, and even if he contracted under duress, nevertheless if uxoricide or a similar danger is not likely to be feared he must be compelled to it by ecclesiastical censure. Otherwise, it would not be medicinal excommunication but deadly, and this ought not to be.[24] Whether by punishing or by pardoning, it is surely only a question of correcting the life of men.[25] Since force is apt to have difficult outcomes, particularly in marriages, the person wishing to withdraw should be admonished rather than forced.[26] It is the same as when a person in mortal sin is not forced to do penance because of the danger that is feared.

Again, if such a one were excommunicated and afterwards contracts with another through words in the present tense, penance should be enjoined on him for the bad faith and obstinacy. He should also be absolved, although he makes no satisfaction for that for which he was excommunicated as he is unable to make satisfaction since the engagement is dissolved because of the

---

[21] RdeP: Extra *de sponsalibus*, "Requisivit" [X 4.1.17], et c. "Gemma" [X 4.1.29].

[22] Text: *pure*

[23] RdeP: Extra *de desponsatione impuberum*, "Accessit" [X 4.2.5].

[24] RdeP: 2 q. 1 "Multi" [*Decretum* C. 2 q.1 c.18].

[25] RdeP: 23 q. 5 "Prodest" [*Decretum* C. 23 q.5 c.4]. And these can be understood in this way: Extra *de sponsalibus*, "Ex litteris" (secundo) [X 4.1.10], and Extra *de desponsatione impuberum*, "Ubi non est consensus" [X 4.2.2].

[26] RdeP: Extra *de sponsalibus*, "Requisivit" [X 4.1.17], "Cum locum" [X 4.1.14]; Extra *de sponsa duorum*, c. ult. [X 4.4.5].

added bond of marriage, which is stronger.[27]

In the other two cases, the one who is of majority age or whoever reaches adulthood first is bound to wait until the minor reaches the legal age for contracting marriage. Then, if the one who was a minor at the time when the engagement was contracted (or both if both were minors) should protest or refuse to consent, they can be separated from each other by a judgment of the Church.[28] Nevertheless, some understand these decretals differently, but what I said seems closer to the truth and the text itself clearly indicates it.

But can one who is already pubescent or of majority age and who con-tracted an engagement or marriage with a pre-pubescent withdraw when the one who was a minor wishes to finalize the marriage on reaching the legal age? You should say no because, from the fact that he once consented to it, he cannot dissent further.[29] Nevertheless, do not understand that the marriage is binding, since it is not whole because there has been no mutual consent. But he is obliged by his promise to contract.

7.    Finally, we must see whether engagements can be dissolved. Note that engagements once contracted always hold and bind in such a way that if an engaged person enters into an engagement afterwards with another he must be compelled to return to the first.[30] This fails in cases in which engagements are dissolved.

The first case is if one of the engaged should transfer to religious life. One can do this before intercourse even if the other is unwilling. The one remaining in the world is released from the engagement bond even if it was an engage-ment about the present.[31]

The second is when one of the engaged is not available because he moved to another region. The woman is free after receiving penance for perjury or for a broken promise if it was her fault that the marriage was not finalized.[32]

The third is if one of the engaged after contracting the engagement catches leprosy or paralysis, or loses eyes or nose, or something more unsightly hap-pens.[33]

The fourth is if affinity arises, for example because the male who was engaged knew a female blood relative of his betrothed, or vice versa.[34] Public

---

[27] RdeP: Extra *de sponsalibus*, "De illis" [X 4.1.5].

[28] RdeP: Extra *de desponsatione impuberum*, "De illis" (primo) [X 4.2.7], "A nobis" [X 4.2.8].

[29] RdeP: Extra *de desponsatione impuberum*, "De illis" (primo) [X 4.2.7].

[30] RdeP: Extra *de sponsalibus*, "Sicut ex litteris" [X 4.1.22].

[31] RdeP: Extra *de conversione coniugatorum*, "Verum" [X 3.32.2], "Ex publico" [X 3.32.7].

[32] RdeP: Extra *de sponsalibus*, "De illis autem" [X 4.1.5].

[33] RdeP: Extra *de coniugio leprosorum*, "Litteras" [X 4.8.3]; Extra *de iureiurando*, "Quemadmod-um" [X 2.24.25].

[34] RdeP: 27 q. 2 "Si quis sponsam filii" [*Decretum* C. 27 q.2 c.32].

report is enough to prove this.[35]

The fifth is if they mutually absolve each other.[36] However, some do not agree with this case and say this is not a decretal or it is understood as comparative permission.[37]

The sixth is if one of them fornicated.[38]

The seventh is when the woman engaged in reference to the future, or the male, contracts with another through words in the present tense, or through words in the future tense and intercourse follows. Then the first engagement is dissolved on account of the greater added bond. But he ought to do penance for bad faith or promise.[39] But what if he simply contracts an engagement in reference to the future with the first and similarly with the second in reference to the future, but an oath is added? I believe that he should return to the first and do penance for the perjury that he committed by swearing an illicit oath. An oath cannot be a bond in an act of iniquity.[40]

The eighth case is when a minor reaches adulthood and asks to be absolved from the engagement bond and to be given freedom to marry another.[41]

And note that all these cases except the first, namely when one wishes to enter religious life, must be understood only of engagements in reference to the future, because then they are truly and unconditionally[42] called engagements. Again, in two of the aforesaid cases engagements are dissolved by the law itself – when one enters religious life, and when marriage is contracted with another man or woman. In the other cases they must be dissolved through a judgment of the Church.

---

[35] RdeP: Extra *de consanguinitate et affinitate*, "Super eo" [X 4.14.2].

[36] RdeP: Extra *de sponsalibus*, "Praeterea" [X 4.1.2].

[37] [X 4.1.2. The idea behind comparative permission is that between two evils one has 'permission' to do the lesser evil to avoid a greater evil. For the expression "comparativa permissio" see *Ordinary Gloss* on Gratian, *Decretum* C. 33 q.2 c.9, ad. v. *adulterium*. The text in question here (X 4.1.2) suggests such permission when it claims that the engagement can be broken off lest there would be a worse result from honouring it, such as hating the wife whom the man marries.]

[38] RdeP: Extra *de iureiurando*, "Quemadmodum" [X 2.24.25].

[39] RdeP: Extra *de sponsalibus*, "Si inter virum" [X 4.1.31]; and *de sponsa duorum*, c. 1 [X 4.4.1].

[40] RdeP: Extra *de iureiurando*, "Quanto" [X 2.24.18]; Extra *de sponsalibus*, "Sicut ex litteris" [X 4.1.22]; 22 q. 4: "Break faith in evil promises. Change the resolve in a shameful vow" [*Decretum* C. 22 q.4 c.5].

[41] RdeP: Extra *de desponsatione impuberum*, "De illis" (primo) [X 4.2.7], et c. "A nobis" [X 4.2.8].

[42] Text: *pure*

# Title II
# Marriage

Now that engagements have been sufficiently discussed, marriage must be dealt with: first: what marriage is; the etymology of the word; how it is contracted; when it was instituted and where and by what words; what the cause of the institution was; who are able to contract marriage; what the goods of marriage are and how they excuse from sin; what the impediments to it are.

1. Marriage is the union of a man and a woman, maintaining an undivided manner of life.[1] Marriage is "of a man and a woman". It does not say "of men and a woman" or "of a man and women" because one man cannot have many wives at once or one woman many husbands.[2] "Union," that is, of souls and matrimonial.[3] "Maintaining an undivided manner of life," that is, neither can profess continence nor give themselves over to prayer without the consent of the other. The marriage bond remains between them while they are living so that neither is permitted to join with another and each offers to the other what he is in himself.[4]

It can also be defined in another way. Marriage is "the union of a man and a woman, a partnership for life, involving divine as well as human law."[5]

It is called "matrimonium" as though "matris munium" (a mother's function), that is, a duty because it confers on women the role of motherhood. Or it receives its name more from the side of the mother than the father because her duty is more apparent in marriage than is the duty of the husband.

2. However, marriage is contracted by consent alone; if this alone is absent all the other celebrations are frustrated even if accompanied by intercourse itself.[6] From the fact that a man consents through words in the present tense to a woman with marital affection, and the woman to the man, either with

---

[1] RdeP: 27 q. 2 § 1 [*Decretum* C. 27 q.2 d.a.c.1]; Extra *de praesumptionibus*, "Illud" [X 2.23.11]; Inst. *de nuptiis*, § 2 [*Inst.* 1.9.1].

[2] RdeP: see below, *De dispari cultu* § "Quid si infidelis" [Title 10.3, p. 00].

[3] RdeP: see below, eodem § "Contrahitur" [Title 2.2, p. 00].

[4] RdeP: see below, eodem § "Effectus" [Title 2.9, 00].

[5] RdeP: ff. *de ritu nuptiarum*, Lex 1 [*Dig.* 23.2.1].

[6] RdeP: Extra *de sponsa duorum*, "Tuas dudum" [X 4.4.5]; 27 q. 2 "Sufficiat" [*Decretum* C. 27 q.2 c.2], "Coniuges verius" [*Decretum* C. 27 q.2 c.6], "Coniux" [*Decretum* C. 27 q.2 c.9].

customary words when he says "I take you as mine" and she replies "I take you as mine" or thus "I wish to have you from now on as my wife" and she says "I wish to have you as my husband," or consent is expressed by some other words or even signs, there is a marriage immediately. I say "signs" because the mute and the deaf can contract marriage.[7] Yet if the contracting parties are able to speak, words expressing mutual consent are necessary as far as the Church is concerned.[8]

3.　It is customary to ask whether this is understood as consent to cohabitation or as consent to carnal copulation.

　　Say that without further distinction[9] it is neither. If it were understood of consent to cohabitation, there would be marriage between a brother and sister, between a son and mother. If it were understood of consent to carnal copulation, there would not have been marriage between Mary and Joseph, for the Blessed Virgin had proposed to remain in virginity unless God should reveal otherwise. So it is understood of matrimonial consent or the consent to conjugal society. This is clear from the formation of the first woman. The Lord did not form her from the man's head lest she seem to be the ruling lady, nor from the feet lest she be considered a servant, but from his side so as to be a companion and friend. Following on this consent or conjugal society they should cohabit and observe an undivided manner of life.[10]

4.　Suppose that someone is engaged to a woman without any intention of contracting marriage but of deceiving so as to be able to extort carnal copulation from her. He then knows her carnally. Will this not count as marriage?

　　In this case there is a diversity of opinion. However, saving a better judgment, it seems to me that he had no intention of marrying her nor did he ever give his consent to her. From this fact there should be no judgment of marriage since the substance of a conjugal contract cannot be found in it. The reason is because deceit alone was present in one party and complete absence of consent without which everything else is incapable of making a conjugal bond.[11] However, if the deceiver wishes to do true penance, he must marry her without deceit as far as it is possible for him, or provide her with a man suitable for her, or otherwise make satisfaction to her in accord with the words of Truth, "If you offer your gift at the altar," etc. (Matt. 5.23).

---

[7] RdeP: Extra *de sponsa duorum*, "Tuas dudum" [X 4.4.5]; Extra *de sponsalibus*, "Si inter" [X 4.1.31], "Cum apud" [X 4.1.23].

[8] RdeP: Extra *de sponsalibus*, "Tuae fraternitatis" [X 4.1.25].

[9] Text: *simpliciter*

[10] RdeP: see above: eodem § "Matrimonium" [above, Title 2.1, p.00]; 27 q. 2 § "Cum ergo" [*Decretum* C. 27 q.2 d.p.c.2].

[11] RdeP: This response is found expressly at: Extra *de sponsalibus*, "Tua nos" [X 4.1.26].

## WHEN MARRIAGE WAS INSTITUTED

5.   Now we must look at when and where and by what words marriage was instituted. It must be said that it was in Paradise and before sin.[12]

By what words was it instituted? Some say with these, "Increase and multiply and fill the earth," etc. (Gen. 1.28), but I do not believe this is true, for these words were rather the blessing of the marriage partners. So it should be said that it was instituted first as a service[13] by Adam's words (uttered prophetically) when he said: "Now this is bone of my bones and flesh of my flesh. For this a man leaves father and mother and clings to his wife and they will be two in one flesh" (Gen. 2.23-24).[14] After sin and outside Paradise marriage was instituted as a remedy to restrain carnal vice.

6.   There are two principal reasons for the institution of marriage, and many secondary reasons. The principal reasons are the raising of children and the avoidance of fornication.[15] Because of the first the Lord instituted marriage in Paradise before sin between the first parents to whom he said, "Increase and multiply" (Gen. 1.28). The second reason is after sin; for this reason the Apostle says, "Because of fornication let each [man] have his own wife and each woman her own husband" (1 Cor. 7.2).

The secondary reasons are many: the maintenance of peace, the wife's beauty, riches, and similar reasons.

But would marriage stand when contracted for such dishonourable reasons as, for example, beauty or riches? Say that it stands, for although the moving reason might be foul or dishonourable, nonetheless it is enough because they intend to contract marriage and they consent to this through words in the present tense.[16] This is also clear from what is read in Genesis, "Jacob seeing that Rachel was beautiful in face and attractive in appearance and loving her he said to Laban, 'I will serve you for seven years for Rachel'" (Gen. 29.17-18). And in Deuteronomy, "If you should see a beautiful woman among the captives and you love her and wish to have her as a wife, you will bring her into your house" (Deut. 21.11-12). An evil life or someone's misguided intention does not contaminate the sacrament of marriage.

---

[12] RdeP: 32 q. 2 § "His ita respondetur" [*Decretum* C. 32 q.2 d.p.c.2].
[13] Text: *ad officium*
[14] RdeP: as is read at: Extra *de divortiis*, "Gaudemus" [X 4.19.8].
[15] RdeP: 32 q. 2 § "His ita" [*Decretum* C. 32 q.2 d.p.c.2].
[16] RdeP: 32 q. 2 "Solet quaeri" [*Decretum* C. 32 q.2 c.6].

## WHO CAN CONTRACT MARRIAGE?

7.    Every person who is able to consent to conjugal affection and union of the flesh can contract marriage, unless expressly prohibited. I said "who is able to consent" because should a boy, although below the lawful age, that is under fourteen, or a girl under twelve, say the words appropriate to contract marriage, nonetheless, because they are not able to consent there is no marriage.[17] A man who lacks both testicles cannot consent.[18] Similarly if a raving man or insane person should say the words he does not contract marriage because he is unable to consent mentally.[19] This is true as long as he is in his raving state, since, if he has a lucid interval and returns to his senses at some time, he is able to marry, and to bear witness, and to do everything that others can do.[20]

    "Unless expressly prohibited" was added because the edict on contracting marriage is prohibitory, that is, everyone who is not prohibited is permited and able to contract.[21] Some are prohibited on account of a vow, orders, and other impediments to be spoken of below.

8.    Can marriage be contracted through proxies between those who are absent? I say it is possible.[22]

## HE WHO CONSENTS TO ONE WHO IS ABSENT

What if someone consents to an absent woman through words in the present tense, then he sends a proxy to her and before she consents in the same way he dissents; afterwards she consents, believing him to continue in his first consent?

    Solution: saving a better judgment, I believe that if he revoked the order and the revocation reached the proxy intact, that is, before the woman consented, nothing happens.[23] If it should arrive after she had already consented, the marriage likewise does not stand because their consents concur neither truly nor interpretatively. If, however, the Church is certain of the first consent of the man, the command to the proxy, and the subsequent consent of the woman, and it is not certain of the aforementioned dissent, the man is bound to finalize the marriage because of the lack of proof. If, however, after he sent

[17] RdeP: Extra *de sponsalibus*, "Tuae fraternitatis" [X 4.1.25].
[18] RdeP: Extra *de frigidis et maleficiatis*, "Quod Sedem" [X 4.15.2].
[19] RdeP:  32 q. 7 "Neque furiosus" [*Decretum* C. 32 q.7 c.26].
[20] RdeP: as it is argued at: 3 q. 9 "Indicas Hermannum" [*Decretum* C. 3 q.9 c.14]; 7 q.1 "Quamvis triste" [*Decretum* C. 7 q.1 c.14]; C. *de codicillis*, "Nec codicillos" [*Code* 6.36.5].
[21] RdeP: Extra *de sponsalibus*, "Cum apud Sedem" [X 4.1.23].
[22] RdeP: 32 q. 2 § "Cum ergo" [*Decretum* C. 32 q.2 d.p.c.12].
[23] RdeP: arg. Extra *de procuratoribus*, "In nostra" [X 1.38.4].

the proxy, he neither consented nor dissented, forgetting because of employment or some other reason, it seems simply to count for marriage both on account of the presumption in favour of marriage and because there is no obstacle posed by a contrary will.[24]

9. One of the effects of marriage is that once there is marriage or matrimony between two people, it never ceases to be even if one of the spouses becomes a heretic.[25] Nor can a husband dismiss his wife should she become leprous or blind or incurr some similar affliction. Nor can a wife dismiss her husband[26] except because of fornication. But if he then dismisses her, he must remain without a wife or be reconciled to his wife.[27]

Again, because the woman does not have power over her own body, but the man, and the man does not have power over his own body, but the woman, another effect is that after carnal copulation follows between them one cannot choose religious life or profess continence if the other is unwilling.[28]

Another effect is that the husband must be compelled to pay the marital debt to his wife even if he has not known her carnally, and she to him, notwithstanding any affinity which has meanwhile sinfully arisen between them.[29]

10. But do spouses sin in demanding or paying the marital debt on solemn feasts, fast days, or in a holy place?

Say to this that the one of whom the demand is made should always pay unless he can put if off cautiously and without the danger of adultery, but he ought not demand during those times. That is why the Apostle says of them, "Do not defraud one another except perhaps for a time by consent that you might give yourselves over to prayer. And return together again lest Satan tempt you because of your incontinence. But I say this by way of indulgence not command" (1 Cor. 7.5-6). And Augustine, "Sometimes it is legitimate for a Christian to come together with his wife, sometimes not, for because of processional days and fasts sometimes it is not legitimate to come together because there should be abstinence even from licit things so that what is required can more easily be accomplished."[30] The same Augustine says, "As often as the

[24] RdeP: Extra de sententia et re iudicata, "Duobus" [ X 2.27.26]; Extra de baptismo et eius effectu, "Maiores" (in fine) [X 3.42.3].

[25] RdeP: 32 q. 7 c.1 et 2 [Decretum C. 32 q.7 c.1-2]; Extra de divortiis, "Quanto" [X 4.19.7].

[26] RdeP: 32 q. 5 "Horrendus" [Decretum C. 32 q.5 c.17], "Si quis uxorem" [Decretum C. 32 q.5 c.18].

[27] RdeP: 32 q. 1 "Dixit Dominus" [Decretum C.32 q.1 c.2].

[28] RdeP: 27 q. 2 "Sunt qui dicunt" [Decretum C. 27 q.2 c.19], "Scripsit nobis" [Decretum C. 27 q.2 c.26]; 33 q. 5 c.1, 2, 3, 4 [Decretum C. 33 q.5 c.1-4].

[29] RdeP: Extra de eo qui cognovit consanguineam uxoris suae, "Discretionem" [X 4.13.6], "Tuae fraternitatis devotio" [X 4.13.10].

[30] [Decretum C. 33 q.4 c.5.]

day of the Nativity or other festivals occur there must be abstinence, not only from union with concubines but also from your own wives."[31]

11. Suppose that a husband accuses his wife of adultery. The wife demands the debt while the case is pending. Is he bound to pay or if he pays spontaneously or even if compelled by the Church, does he become irregular so that from then on he could not be promoted?

Solution: regarding the first I distinguish: either it was publicly known that she was an adulteress or it was not. In the first case he ought neither to pay nor demand the debt unless she wishes to refrain and to do penance,[32] or unless he himself fornicated; then equal crimes are removed by equal compensation.[33] Again Augustine, "Nothing is more iniquitous than to dismiss one's wife if he too was convicted of fornicating. For this passage comes to mind, 'In what you judge another, you condemn yourself'," etc. (Rom. 2.1).[34] In the second case he ought to pay the one asking because he ought not to despoil her before the judgment.[35]

But after adultery has been committed does she by the law itself lose the right of demanding the debt of the continent? It seems so, at least as far as the judgment of the soul, because by sinning against the law of marriage she renders herself unworthy, and so she ought not ask unless the fault has been purged by penance. But if she asks he ought to pay, as was said.

To the question whether he becomes irregular if he pays the debt in those circumstances, I believe that he does.[36]

12. The goods of marriage are principally three: fidelity, offspring, sacrament. Whence Augustine: "The nuptial good is three-fold: fidelity, offspring, sacrament. In fidelity care is taken that after the marriage bond there be no intercourse with another man or woman. In offspring, that the offspring be lovingly raised and religiously educated. In sacrament, that the marriage not be dissolved."[37] Although bodily separation sometimes occurs because of fornication or by mutual consent for prayer or religious life, sacramental separation is not

---

[31] [*Decretum* C. 33 q.4 c.2.]

[32] RdeP: 32 q.1 c.1, 2, 3, 4, et sex capitulis sequentibus [*Decretum* C. 32 q.1 c.1-10]; Extra *de divortiis*, "Significasti" [X 4.19.4]; et *de adulteriis*, "Si vir" [X 5.16.3].

[33] RdeP: Extra *de divortiis*, "Significasti" [X 4.19.4]; Extra *de adulteriis*, c. paenult. et ult. [X 5.16.6-7].

[34] RdeP: 32 q. 6 "Nihil" et quattuor capitulis sequentibus [*Decretum* C. 32 q.6 c.1-5].

[35] RdeP: Extra *de divortiis*, "Porro" [X 4.19.3]; Extra *ut lite pendente*, "Laudabilem" [X 2.16.2]; 8 q. 4 "Nonne" [*Decretum* C. 8 q.4 c.1].

[36] RdeP: see *Summa de paenitentia*, in titulo De bigamis § "Item quid si maritus" [Raymond, *Summa de paenitentia* 3.3.5 (ed. Ochoa and Díez, col. 582)].

[37] [See Augustine, *The Literal Meaning of Genesis*, translated by John H. Taylor, vol. 2 (Books 7-12), Ancient Christian Writers 42 (New York, 1982) 9.7.12 (p. 78).]

possible unless the matrimonial bond ceases, which never happens between the faithful unless through entry into religious life before carnal copulation or, after carnal copulation through the death of both spouses or one of them.

Are these three so necessary that if one of them is absent the marriage would not stand? To this say that if at the time of the contract they intend to observe them, even though afterwards they do otherwise after changing their wills, the marriage stands nonetheless.[38] I say the same if they do not think of these goods, for it is enough that they do not propose a condition or agreement to do the contrary.[39]

Again, note that the good of offspring does not mean offspring itself, which is sometimes sought on account of hereditary succession, but the hope and desire to have children so that they might be shaped by religion. So, many have offspring, who do not have the good of offspring, but the marriage does not cease for that reason.

Again, note that the third good of marriage is called sacrament, not that it is the marriage itself but because it is a sign of a holy thing itself, that is, of the spiritual and inseparable union of Christ and the Church.

It is clear from the foregoing that the first two goods sometimes accompany marriage, sometimes do not, but the third adheres inseparably as long as the marriage lasts.

13. These goods are capable of excusing from sin if the spouses come together for offspring and the fidelity of the marriage bed is observed. So note that sometimes spouses come together to have children, sometimes to pay the debt, sometimes because of incontinence or to avoid fornication, sometimes to satisfy lust. In the first and second cases there is no sin; in the third, venial sin; in the fourth, mortal sin.

Of the first, Augustine, "Conjugal intercourse for the sake of procreation is without sin."[40] The Apostle, "If a virgin marries she does not sin" (1 Cor. 7.28). If there could be no conjugal intercourse without sin, after the flood the Lord would not have ordered them to copulate, saying in Genesis, "Increase and multiply" (Gen. 9.7), since by that time they were unable to be united without carnal concupiscence.

Of the second, Augustine, "Pay the debt, and if you do not ask, pay. God will count it for your perfect sanctification if you do not demand what is due you, but you pay what you owe your wife."

Of the third, Augustine, "Perhaps someone will say, if the Apostle grants

---

[38] RdeP: see above, eodem § "Effectus." [Title 2.9].

[39] RdeP: see below, *De impedimento conditionis* § ult. [Title 4.3].

[40] [Augustine, *The Good of Marriage*, translated by C. T. Wilcox, The Fathers of the Church 27 (New York, 1955) 6.6 (p. 17).]

forgiveness, therefore marriage is a sin, for to whom is forgiveness granted except to a sinner?" Further on, "While granting forgiveness the Apostle has an eye to intercourse of the married where there is the evil of incontinence. The evil of incontinence is when a husband knows his wife even beyond the necessity of procreating children. But the good of marriage is also there." And further, "This good is not culpable on account of that evil, but that evil is made venial on account of the marriage good."[41]

Of the fourth, the Philosopher, "The too ardent lover of his own wife is an adulterer."[42] And Jerome,[43] "The wise man loves his wife with judgment, not feeling; the impetus for pleasure does not reign in him nor is he borne precipitously to intercourse. For nothing is more foul than to love one's wife as an adulteress."[44]

14. Again, note that marriage is lawful or clandestine. Lawful is when a wife is sought from those who have power over the woman, is promised by the parents, is endowed according to the laws, is blessed by the priests as is customary, is watched over by the bridesmaids, and is solemnly received. Otherwise, marriage is not presumed but it is called adultery or fornication;[45] then it is called clandestine.

Nonetheless, you should not understand that there cannot be a true marriage without such solemnities, but the canon speaks according to what the Church presumes in the absence of proof. Or say that in this sacrament as in others there are things pertaining to the substance such as consent about the present, which alone suffices.[46] Then there are things pertaining to adornment and uprightness such as the aforesaid solemnities, without which there is true and lawful marriage as to the truth of the matter, but not as to uprightness.

So these people should be counselled in the forum of penance to give their consent anew or to acknowledge and approve publicly before the Church what they did in secret, and to do penance because they scandalized the Church and exposed themselves to great danger. One could dismiss the other when he

---

[41] [These three texts attributed to Augustine about the third reason for intercourse are likely from Peter Lombard, *Sent.*, 4, D. 31.6.3; 4, D. 31.6.3 to 7.1; 4, D. 31.7.1 (p. 448). The editors of Lombard's *Sentences* claim that the only source for the first two texts is Lombard's commentary on 1 Cor. 7.6 (PL 176.1598A-B). For the third text see Augustine, *The Literal Meaning of Genesis* 9.7.12 (Taylor, tr., pp. 77-78).]

[42] [*Decretum* C. 32 q.4 c.5, § 1. For an account of this text see Pierre J. Payer, *The Bridling of Desire. Views of Sex in the Later Middle Ages* (Toronto, 1993) pp. 120-128.]

[43] [*Decretum* C. 32 q.4 c.5, § 1.]

[44] RdeP: For everything I have said about the goods of marriage you will find at: 32 q. 2 per totum [*Decretum* C. 32, q.2] and q. 4 "Origo" [*Decretum* C. 32 q.4 c.5]; et in libro quarto *Sententiarum* in tractatu *De matrimonio* [P. Lombard, *Sent.* 4, D. 31 (pp. 442-451)].

[45] RdeP: 30 q. 5 "Aliter" [*Decretum* C. 30 q.5 c.1].

[46] RdeP: see above, eodem § "Contrahitur." [Title 2.2].

wished and contract marriage with still another as a matter of fact and, because of a failure of proof, remain with impunity in adultery as regards the Church militant.

15. Again, marriage is sometimes called initiated, sometimes completed[47] or consummated. It is called initiated through consent expressed in the present tense;[48] completed, however, or consummated through carnal copulation.[49]

But according to this it seems that there was no completed marriage between the Blessed Virgin and Joseph, which is the height of absurdity to say. Therefore, say that it was a true marriage. So Augustine, "Blessed Mary proposed that she would remain a virgin unless God should reveal otherwise to her. Therefore, committing her virginity to divine disposition, she consented to carnal copulation, not in desiring it but in obeying divine inspiration as to either possibility. Afterwards she gave oral expression to this together with her husband and both remained in virginity."[50] Again, Augustine says there was a completed marriage between them; completed, not in signification but in holiness. Thus when writing to a woman who had made a vow of chastity together with her husband, he says among other things, "He did not cease being your husband because you both refrained from carnal union. In fact, the more you observed the holier agreements in harmony, the holier you remained as spouses."[51] That marriage was also completed because of the three-fold good of marriage. Augustine again, "So every marriage good was fulfilled in those parents of Christ – offspring, fidelity, and sacrament. We know the offspring – the Lord himself; fidelity, because there was no adultery; sacrament, because there was no divorce. Marital intercourse alone was not there because it cannot occur in the flesh of sin without the shameful concupiscence of the flesh that results from sin. He who would be without sin wished to be conceived without such concupiscence."[52]

It is clear from this that a marriage is called completed or consummated through holiness, even before carnal copulation, as was said. However, it is said to be completed in signification through carnal copulation. Since it is a sacrament it is a holy sign of a holy thing, that is, of the union of Christ and the Church, as the Apostle says, "A man leaves father and mother and will cling to his wife and they will be two in one flesh. This is a great sacrament; but I speak in reference to Christ and the Church" (Eph. 5.30-31). For just as

---

[47] Text: *perfectum*

[48] RdeP: 27 q. 2 "Cum initiatur" [*Decretum* C. 27 q.2 c.5], "Coniuges" [*Decretum* C. 27 q.2 c.6].

[49] RdeP: Extra *de bigamis*, "Debitum" [X 1.21.5].

[50] RdeP: 27 q. 2 § "Cum ergo" [*Decretum* C. 27 q.2 d.p.c.2].

[51] RdeP: 33 q. 4 "Quod Deo" [*Decretum* C. 33 q.5 c.4].

[52] [*Decretum* C. 27 q.2 c.10.]

there is a union of souls and bodies between spouses, so the Church is joined to Christ in will and nature because it wills the same as he, and he assumed human nature. So the bride is joined to the bridegroom spiritually and bodily, that is, by charity and the conformity of nature.[53]

Some also say of marriage: initiated through engagement expressed in the future tense; ratified through consent expressed in the present tense; consummated through carnal copulation.

Again, there is lawful and not ratified marriage; another, ratified and not lawful another, lawful and ratified.

Lawful marriage is what is contracted according to legal institution or provincial custom, not contrary to the Lord's command. And this is even between unbelievers among whom there is no ratified marriage because it occurs without faith. What Augustine says is to be understood in this way, "What is without God is not a ratified marriage."[54]

Ratified and not lawful marriage is between believers, lawful persons but contracted without lawful solemnity.[55] Note, that this is ratified marriage because indissoluble.[56]

Lawful and ratified marriage is between believers if contracted with due solemnity. This distinction is proven.[57]

16. Finally, we must look at what the impediments to marriage are and how many there are. It should be known that there are only twelve impediments that impede marriage from being contracted and break off what is already contracted if any of them preceded the marriage, since they exclude marital consent. If, however, they follow the marriage, they offer no impediment, as is clear from the following examples. A raving mad person cannot contract marriage, yet if it was contracted before the madness, the marriage is not dissolved.[58] Again, if one is completely castrated, he cannot contract marriage, but if he is castrated after marriage, the marriage is not dissolved.[59] Again, affinity impedes marriage from being contracted and breaks off what is already contracted. But if it comes after marriage has been contracted, even if carnal copulation between the spouses did not follow, the marriage is not dissolved and

---

[53] RdeP: for this see *Summa de paenitentia*, in titulo de bigamis [Raymond, *Summa de paenitentia* 3.3 (ed. Ochoa and Díez, col. 577)].

[54] [*Decretum* C. 28 q.1 d.p.c.17. See note to Peter Lombard, *Sent.*, 4, D. 39.5.3 (p. 489).]

[55] RdeP: see above, eodem, § 5 [Title 2.14, p. 00].

[56] RdeP: see above, eodem, § "Effectus." [Title 2.9].

[57] RdeP: 28 q.1 § "Item illud Augustini" [*Decretum* C. 28 q.1 d.p.c.17]; Extra *de divortiis*, "Quanto" [X 4.19.7], "Gaudemus" [X 4.19.8].

[58] RdeP: 32 q. 7 "Neque furiosus" [*Decretum* C. 32 q.7 c.26].

[59] RdeP: 32 q. 7 "Illi qui sani" [*Decretum* C. 32 q.7 c.25].

the husband is bound to pay the debt to his wife.[60] The same is to be understood of all the other impediments

> What the impediments are is contained in four short verses:
> Error, condition, vow, relationship, crime.
> Disparity of religion, force, orders, bond, honesty.
> If you are related by affinity, if you are incapable of coitus.
> These prohibit marriage from being formed, undo formed unions.

Beyond these twelve impediments, which impede and break off marriage, there are two other impediments that impede from contracting marriage but do not break off what has been contracted. They are feast days and the prohibition of the Church. Hence the verses:

> Church prohibitions and celebrations
> Impede from happening, permit what has been done to endure.

How it should be understood will be spoken of in what follows.

---

[60] RdeP: Extra *de eo qui cognovit consanguineam uxoris suae*, "Discretionem" [X 4.13.6].

# Title III
## Error about a Person

After indicating what the impediments are and their number, we continue more extensively with each in order.

1.  First, the impediment of error about a person. Unlike several impediments, it excludes consent by its very nature, not through the regulation of the Church, since whoever errs does not consent,[1] and the will of the one in error is of no account.[2] So, if a woman or man errs in contracting marriage, there is no consent, which alone makes a marriage. Thus, in its absence there is no marriage; and this is expressly proven.[3]

Note that for a man, or for a woman to err in consenting to a man whom she thinks is someone else, it is necessary that through sight, hearing, or reputation she have some knowledge of the absent person whom she believes this present person to be. The reason for this is that we cannot direct our affection or consent towards someone completely unknown.[4] So, as was said, when one consents to an absent person somewhat known to him, whom he thinks is present, it is clear that he does not consent to the person who is present, but to the person who is thought to be present. And so there is no marriage when one errs about a person.

But if a woman has no knowledge of the absent person, she does not err regarding that person but is deceived about the one present. For example, if some rustic Englishman approaches a noble woman saying he is the son of the king of England (who is unknown to the woman) and she contracts marriage with him believing him to be the son of the king, the marriage is not impeded because there was no error about the person. Rather, there was error about the quality, which does not impede, just as error regarding fortune does not impede.[5]

---

[1] RdeP: ff. *de iurisdictione omnium iudicum*, "Si per errorem" [*Dig.* 2.1.15].

[2] RdeP: C. *de iuris et facti ignorantia*, "Cum per testamentum" [*Code* 1.18.8], "Non idcirco" [*Code* 1.18.9].

[3] RdeP: 29 q. 1 § "His ita" [*Decretum* C. 29 q.1 § 1].

[4] RdeP: ff. *de contrahenda emptione*, "Cum ab eo, § Mensam" [*Dig.* 18.1.41, 1].

[5] RdeP: 29 q. 1 § "His ita" [*Decretum* C. 29 q.1 § 1].

2.   There is said to be error of quality when one is thought to be good or noble or a virgin and such like, and he is evil or ignoble or corrupted, and vice versa. Error of fortune is when one is believed to be rich and is poor.

# Title IV
## The Impediment of Condition

The examination of the impediment of condition, that is, of servitude, follows. This impediment was introduced by the Church in favour of liberty.

1.    Concerning it, briefly it should be known that if a free woman knowingly contracts with a slave or a free man with a female slave, the marriage stands.[1] But if a free woman contracts marriage with a slave unknowingly, believing him to be free, or a free man with a female slave believing her to be free, there is no marriage.[2] This means that there is no marriage between them unless, after he learns of her real condition, he consents to her orally or in deed, namely, through carnal copulation.[3]

   Again, note that an error about a worse condition, namely, a servile condition, impedes a marriage from being contracted and breaks off what has already been contracted, but not an error about an equal or a better condition; for example, if a slave unknowingly contracts marriage with a female slave whom he believes to be free or a free woman whom he believes to be a female slave, because he is not deceived nor does he have anything that he might object to.[4] Again, another reason is because such a decree is prohibitory, that is, whoever is not prohibited is permitted.

2.    What if marriages are contracted between slaves and their masters are opposed or unwilling? Say that they are not to be dissolved for that reason. However, they ought to show no less due and customary service to their own masters.[5]

   Suppose the master orders the married slave to do something and at the same time his wife asks for the debt, or vice versa. Saving a better judgment, I believe a distinction must be made, since the slave contracted marriage either

   [1] RdeP: 29 q. 2 "Si quis liber" [*Decretum* C. 29 q.2 c.2], "Si quis ancillam" [*Decretum* C. 29 q.2 c.3].

   [2] RdeP: 29 q. 2 "Si quis ingenuus" [*Decretum* C. 29 q.2 c.4], "Si femina ingenua" [*Decretum* C. 29 q.2 c.5].

   [3] RdeP: 29 q. 2 "Si quis ingenuus" [*Decretum* C. 29 q.2 c.4], "Si femina ingenua" [*Decretum* C. 29 q.2 c.5]; Extra *de coniugio servorum*, "Proposuit" [X 4.9.2], "Ad nostram" [X 4.9. 4].

   [4] RdeP: arg. 32 q. 6 per totum [*Decretum* C. 32 q.6]; Extra *de divortiis*, "Significasti" [X 4.19.4].

   [5] RdeP: Extra *de coniugio servorum*, c. 1 [ X 4.9.1].

with the consent of his master or the master did not know or was opposed. In the first case, he ought to pay the debt since, because the master gave his consent to the main matter, that is, to the marriage, he is understood to have granted permission for those things that are connected with the marriage contract.[6] In the second case, however, it seems that he ought to carry out the master's order unless he fears a probable danger of adultery from the delay; otherwise, the master could be deprived of the service of his slave without any fault of his own, which ought not to be.[7] What I noted about the monk, the wife, and the family son suggests this solution;[8] also what I noted of the slave whose ordination is unknown to the master, or known to him and he opposes or he consents.[9]

3.   A distinction must be made in regard to conditions added to engagements. The condition is either licit or illicit. Again, if licit, it is either necessary or voluntary. If it is foul or illicit, a further subdistinction: either it is contrary to the substance or nature of marriage, or it is not.

A licit and necessary condition is one where, if not introduced, the action is null.[10]

A licit and voluntary condition is one that can be introduced or not, such as "I shall contract marriage with you if my father is willing" or "if you will give me a hundred marks." If this is added, it suspends the engagement until the condition is met. This is so even if an oath should intervene, unless in the meantime consent expressed in the present tense or carnal copulation should have followed. The reason for this is because then a true marriage is said to exist between them since they seem to have withdrawn from the proposed condition.[11]

A condition that is illicit and is against the nature or substance of marriage is when he says "I contract with you if you avoid the generation of offspring" or "until I should find another woman more worthy in honour and attributes" or "if you give yourself over to adultery for gain." If this is added, the action is nullified.[12]

---

[6] RdeP: Extra *de officio delegati*, "Praeterea" (in fine) [X 1.29.5].

[7] RdeP: see above, § proximo [Title 4.2, p. 00].

[8] RdeP: see *Summa de paenitentia*, in titulo *De negotiis saecularibus*, § "Sed quaeritur circa hoc" et quinque § sequentibus [Raymond, *Summa de paenitentia* 2.8.8-12 (ed. Ochoa and Díez, col. 567-574)].

[9] RdeP: see *Summa de paenitentia*, in titulo De servis non ordinandis, § "Si servus" [Raymond, *Summa de paenitentia* 3.17.3 (ed. Ochoa and Díez, col. 619)].

[10] RdeP: for this see below, *De dispari cultu*, in principio [Title 10].

[11] RdeP: Extra *de conditionibus appositis in desponsatione*, "De illis" [X 4.5.3] "Super eo" [X 4.5.5], "Per tuas" [X 4.5.6].

[12] RdeP: 22 q. 4 "Inter cetera" [*Decretum* C. 22 q.4 c.22]; 32 q. 2 "Aliquando" [*Decretum* C. 32

A condition that is illicit but not against the nature of marriage is when one says, "I will contract marriage with you, if you steal," "if you murder a man." If this is added, it is to be broken or not considered as having been added, and the engagement or marriage stands.[13]

q.2 c.7]; "Solet quaeri" [*Decretum* C. 32 q.2 c.6]; Extra *de conditionibus appositis in desponsatione*, c. ult. [X 4.5.7].

[13] RdeP: Extra *de conditionibus appositis*, c. 1 et ult. [X 4.5.1 and 7].

# Title V
## The Impediment of Vow

The impediment of vow must be dealt with next. However, since many have said many different things on this point, for a fuller understanding of what should be held we must examine: what a vow is; who can vow; at what age does a vow hold; the species of vow; what vow breaks off a marriage already contracted.

1.  A vow is described in this way: a vow is a promise of a good made with deliberation;[1] or: a vow is the conception of a proposed good strengthened with deliberation by which one obliges oneself to God to do or not to do something. Although vows are diverse according to the diversity of the things vowed, nonetheless a vow of continence impedes and breaks off a marriage.

2.  Let us see who can vow. And it should be known that anyone of sane mind can vow unless expressly prohibited, since a vow is inspired by the law of the Holy Spirit.

Spouses, however, are prohibited from making a vow of continence unless by mutual consent and will, and one cannot enter religious life without the consent of the other. If one vows without the consent of the other or even enters a monastery, he can be recalled by the other spouse. This applies after carnal copulation; for before carnal copulation, even if the marriage was contracted between them through words in the present tense, either of them can enter religious life with the other unwilling and forbidding it. The one remaining in the world can contract another marriage.

Again, a slave cannot vow or choose monastic life if the master is unwilling.

Again, if boys or girls make a vow before the time of puberty (fourteen for a boy, twelve for a girl), a father or guardian can revoke it without sin.

I said "of sane mind" since, if a man with a mental aberration should make a vow or enter a monastery, the vow does not hold.[2] Aside from those persons,

---

[1] RdeP: see *Summa de paenitentia*, in eodem titulo, § 1 [see Raymond, *Summa de paenitentia* 1.8.1 (ed. Ochoa and Díez, col. 339)].

[2] RdeP: Extra *de regularibus et transeuntibus ad religionem*, "Sicut tenor" [X 3.31.15].

I believe that all others can make a solemn vow.[3]

3.   Next, at what age can a vow be solemnized? It should be known that the legitimate age for a woman is twelve, fourteen for a male. So, if they pronounce a solemn vow after that age or if what they pronounced as minors they did not revoke when they reached the legal age, afterwards a vow or monastic profession will remain firm and ratified.[4]

4.   Now we must look at how many species of vow there are. There are two—simple vow and solemn vow.

A simple vow is one that is simply pronounced without the use of any solemnity, as when one says "I vow continence," "I wish to be a monk," and goes no further.

A solemn vow is when a solemnity follows the vow. Note that some say of this solemnity or solemnizing that a vow is solemnized in three ways: through one's own profession, through holy orders, through the reception of a habit. But some canons expressly say that a habit without profession does not make a monk, and impedes from contracting marriage but does not break off one already contracted.[5] Therefore, they distinguish three habits: probation, which has no vow annexed;[6] conversion, which has a vow of continence annexed,[7] but not a solemn vow; profession, which has a solemn vow annexed.[8]

Those who say this appear to argue subtly, but the diversity of habits that they propose is neither proven by law nor demonstrated in the outward appearance of different habits. So I believe with others that a habit alone, unless something else follows or is presumed, does not solemnize a vow, but true or presumed profession alone makes a monastic solemn vow, as in the two decretals alleged previously.[9] I said "presumed" because if, in a monastery, one takes the habit that is customarily given to those making profession, or if

---

[3] RdeP: see *Summa de paenitentia*, in eodem titulo, § "Potest autem votum, versu Potestate vero superiori," usque ad § "Sequitur videre" [Raymond, *Summa de paenitentia* 1.8.5-8 (ed. Ochoa and Díez, col. 345-351); 1.8.12-16 (col. 357-361)].

[4] RdeP: 20 q. 1 "Illud" [*Decretum* C. 20 q.1 c.10], et q. 2 c. 1 et 2 [*Decretum* C. 20 q.2 c.1-2]; Extra *de regularibus et transeuntibus ad religionem*, "Ad nostram" [X 3.31.8], "Significatum" [X 3.31.11], "Cum simus" [X 3.31.14]. For this see *Summa de paenitentia*, in eodem titulo, § "Potest autem votum versu Item impuberes" [Raymond, *Summa de paenitentia* 1.8.7 (ed. Ochoa and Díez, col. 347)].

[5] RdeP: Extra *de regularibus et transeuntibus*, "Porrectum" [X 3.31.13]; Extra *qui clerici vel voventes*, "Consuluit" [X 4.6.4].

[6] RdeP: in which case they refer to: Extra *de renuntiatione*, "Ex transmissa" [X 1.9.3]

[7] RdeP: in this case they understand this decretal: *Qui clerici vel voventes* "Consuluit" [X 4.6.4].

[8] RdeP: and this is how they understand the chapter. 27 dist. "Quod interrogasti" [*Decretum* D. 27 c.6]; Extra *de regularibus et transeuntibus*, "Super eo" [X 3.31.9], "Vidua" [X 3.31.4].

[9] RdeP: "Consuluit" [X 4.6.4] and "Porrectum" [X 3.31.13].

the habit of the professed is not different from the habit of novices, yet he acts in the choir, chapter, and refectory like a monk, he is presumed to have made profession.[10] The result is that even if he should wish to swear that he was not accepted in the sense that he would remain there perpetually, he is not to be heard.[11]

However, if he receives the habit outside the monastery, he is not presumed to have made profession nor to have solemnized a vow, but he is only presumed to have made a simple vow.[12] If, however, he receives the habit in his own home and vows in the hand of a public person, he is judged to have solemnized his vow so that if he contracts marriage, he is to be separated.[13] This is because of the profession he made and not because of the habit, otherwise it would be contrary to the decretal *Consuluit*.[14] So, without any doubt I believe that it must be said that true or presumed profession alone makes a monastic vow solemn.

5.   What about those who have worn a monastic or regular habit for a long time but nonetheless have their own property and otherwise live ordinarily, saying they are not bound to be without their own property or to continence and other observances of a rule because the habit does not make the monk but profession according to a rule? Say that such people, who have no fear of making their way on earth along two paths in the aforesaid manner, are to be compelled through their bishops by ecclesiastical censure to profess and obey a rule according to the form of a religious order after they have worn the habit for a year.[15]

Again, a vow is solemnized through the reception of holy orders.[16]

6.   It follows that a vow impedes matrimony. It must be said that a simple vow impedes the contracting of marriage to such an extent that if the one who made a simple vow afterwards professed an oath that he would take a woman as his wife, he ought to fulfil the vow and do penance for the illicitly made oath.[17] If the one making a simple vow afterwards contracts through words in

---

[10] RdeP: dist. 27 "Quod interrogasti" [*Decretum* D. 27 c.6].

[11] RdeP: Extra *de regularibus*, "Vidua" [X 3.31.4]. See for this: *Summa de paenitentia*, § "Quaeritur circa votum" et duobus § sequentibus [Raymond, *Summa de paenitentia* 1.8.10-12 (ed. Ochoa and Díez, col. 353-357)].

[12] RdeP: Extra *qui clerici vel voventes*, "Consuluit" [X 4.6.4]; Extra *de regularibus*, "Porrectum" [X 3.31.13].

[13] RdeP: Extra *qui clerici vel voventes*, "Insinuante" [X 4.6.7].

[14] [X 4.6.7.]

[15] RdeP: Extra *de regularibus*, "Ex parte" [X 3.31.22].

[16] RdeP: see *Summa de paenitentia*, in eodem titulo, § "Item quid si maritus" [Raymond, *Summa de paenitentia* 1.8.15 (ed. Ochoa and Díez, col. 358)].

[17] RdeP: Extra *qui clerici vel voventes*, "Rursus" [X 4.6.6].

the present tense, the marriage stands.[18] A solemn vow impedes the contracting of marriage, and breaks off one already contracted.[19]

For the sake of brevity, what has been said of vows should suffice.

---

[18] RdeP: dist. 27 "Si vir" [*Decretum* D. 27 c.3], and in the previously alleged decretal, "Rursus" [X 4.6.6].

[19] RdeP: dist. 27 "Voventibus" [*Decretum* D. 27 c.4]; 27 q. 1 fere per totum [*Decretum* C. 27 q.1]; Extra *qui clerici vel voventes*, "Meminimus" [X 4.6.3].

# Title VI
## Carnal Relationship

After the treatment of the impediment of vow, we must examine the impediment of relationship.

In this regard it should be known that relationship is three-fold: carnal, spiritual, and legal. Because carnal relationship, which is called consanguinity, naturally precedes the other two, we shall examine it first. Although many and varied things have been written about consanguinity by the doctors and our betters in the explanation of the tree of consanguinity and of different canons, which on the surface seem to be contrary, nonetheless, in many matters little useful has been compiled that relates to the present teaching. So we must examine: what consanguinity is; what is the derivation of the word; what a line of consanguinity is and how many there are; what a degree[1] is; how degrees are computed and to what degree marriage is prohibited.

1.  Consanguinity is the bond contracted by carnal propagation between persons who descend from the same trunk. I call the trunk the person from whom others take their origin, as Adam was the trunk of Cain and Abel and the children who proceeded from them.

2.  Consanguinity is from "con" (with) and "sanguine" (blood), as if having common blood or as proceeding from one blood.

A line is an ordered collection of persons joined by consanguinity, descending from the same trunk, embracing different degrees.

There are three lines: of those ascending, descending, and transverse or collateral, just as the diversity of near or consanguine relations is three-fold.

The first is of those ascending from whom we take our origin: as father, mother; grandfather, grandmother; great grandfather, great grandmother; great great grandfather, great great grandmother.

The second is of those descending, who take their origin from us: as son, daughter; grandson, granddaughter; great grandson, great granddaughter; great great grandson, great great granddaughter.

The other is of those from the transverse position or of those coming from the side, from whom we neither take our origin nor they from us: as

[1] Text: *gradus*

brother, sister; sons of two brothers called cousins on the father's side,[2] or sons of two sisters who are called cousins on the mother's side;[3] and their children and grandchildren.[4]

Note that two descending lines make one transverse line as is seen in this example: sons of two brothers are related to each other in the transverse line, and each of them descends in a straight line from their common grandfather, who was the common trunk from whom they took their origin. The same is to be understood of all others, both the more remote and the closer.

3.   Next we examine what degree is. For this, note that a degree is described in different ways according to different computations, namely civil and canonical. According to the civil laws, any person establishes a degree. According to the canons, in the transverse line two people establish a degree, so that, for example, two brothers are in the first degree according to the canons. They are in the second degree according to the laws. Sons of two brothers are in the second, but they are in the fourth according to the laws, and so of each.

This diversity of computations and definitions is found in the explanation of certain canons and in the doctrine of the tree. But in regard to the matter at hand, that is, when consanguinity must be computed to join or disjoin a marriage, because persons must be counted from both sides as one proceeds from the other and degrees are to be distinguished from both sides,[5] the following definition suffices.

4.   A degree is the relationship between distant persons whereby it is known by how much generational distance they differ between themselves.

Degree is computed in the following way. In the ascending line: father and mother are in the first degree; grandfather and grandmother in the second; great grandfather, great grandmother in the third; great great grandfather, great great grandmother in the fourth.

In the descending line they are computed in this way: son, daughter in the first degree; grandson, granddaughter in the second degree; great grandson, great granddaughter in the third; great great grandson, great great granddaughter in the fourth.

In the transverse line they are computed thus: according to the canons two brothers are in the first degree; sons of two brothers in the second; their grandchildren in the third; great grandchildren in the fourth. No consanguinity goes beyond this degree today, just as in the past it did not go beyond the seventh

[2] Text: *fratres patrueles*

[3] Text: *fratres consobrini*

[4] RdeP: as is expressly noted: 35 q. 5 "Primo gradu" [*Decretum* C. 35 q.5 c.6].

[5] RdeP: Extra *de consanguinitate et affinitate*, "Ex litteris" (in fine) [X 4.14.1], "Quod dilectio" [X 4.14.3].

degree.[6] But according to the laws two brothers are in the second degree; their children in the fourth, and so they are doubled in each degree.

After these computations, both according to the civil laws and the canons, we must see how consanguinity is to be found and computed between persons. When you want to know of the consanguinity of certain people in terms of how they differ between themselves, run back to the common person from whom they took their origin. For example: Peter fathered Seius and Titus, who were brothers – this is the first degree. If indeed it is not possible to know who their father was, say, "Seius and Titus were brothers." I say this because brothers are always to be placed in the first degree, or brother and sister, or two sisters.

Then proceed with the computation: Seius and Titus were brothers, who, as was said, constitute the first degree. Again Seius fathered A, the second degree; A gave birth to B, the third; B gave rise to C, the fourth, of whom [male] it is now a question. Now return to the other brother and proceed thus: Titus and Seius were brothers and in the first degree, as was said. Titus fathered G, the second degree; G gave birth to H, of whom [female] it is now a question, and so you have the third degree. In this way these two, husband and wife, are usually said to relate to each other on one part in the third degree, but on the other in the fourth. I say "usually" because they are not related to each other truly in the third degree, but in the fourth degree alone,[7] and it is clear in the doctrine of the tree.[8] The same must be done regarding those who are closer in consanguinity and it must be said: they are related in such and such a degree.

That degrees are to be distinguished and computed in this way, and the persons named with their own or equivalent names (the computation starting from the trunk, that is, from the parents or from those having the same parents) is expressly gathered from two decretals.[9]

But suppose some persons are related to each other on the one part in the

[6] RdeP: 35 q. 5 "Ad Sedem" [*Decretum* C. 35 q.5 c.2].

[7] RdeP: see below, eodem, § proximo [Title 6.4, p. 00].

[8] ["The doctrine of the tree" refers to a common way of representing degrees and lines of consanguinity and affinity. Early in the thirteenth century Robert of Flamborough suggests the purpose of the tree, "On account of the great intricacy that is found here in consanguinity and affinity it is necessary here to have a tree of consanguinity and affinity in hand and before the eyes." *Liber poenitentialis*, a critical edition with introduction and notes, edited by J. J. Francis Firth, Studies and Texts 18 (Toronto, 1971) book 2.42 (p. 80). Unfortunately, Firth does not reproduce the tree Robert says he appended to his work. For an example of such reproductions see, *Corpus iuris canonici. 1. Decretum Magistri Gratiani*, edited by E. Friedberg (Leipzig, 1879; rpt. 1959) col. 1425-26 (tree of consanguinity), 1431-32 (tree of affinity); Gerhard Ladner, "Medieval and Modern Understanding of Symbolism: A Comparison," *Speculum* 54 (1979): 240-250 and figures 13-17.]

[9] RdeP: Extra *de consanguinitate*, "Tua nos" [X 4.14.7]; Extra *de testibus*, "Licet ex quadam" [X 2.20.47].

second or third degree, and on the other part in the fifth according to the
computation I demonstrated above. Are they able to contract marriage?

You should say yes because the relationship of the person in the further
degree of consanguinity always prevails.[10] In this case the further person is
beyond the limit of consanguinity and is not related to him because there is no
relation of consanguinity. Just as in the past all consanguinity terminated in the
seventh degree,[11] so today all consanguinity terminates in the fourth degree, at
least as regards the prohibition of conjugal union. Nor should you be influ-
enced by what Isidore says,[12] that is, that all consanguinity terminates in six
degrees, since he locates the first degree in the sons of two brothers, where we
locate the second. So what, according to those laws and computations, were
the sixth for him would be the seventh for us, and what today according to the
same computation would be the third for him, would be the fourth for us.

5.    Finally, we must examine up to what degree someone is prohibited from
taking a wife of his own consanguine line. And it should be said, up to the
fourth degree so that if someone should presume to marry against this prohibition, no length of time is a defence since duration of time does not diminish
but increases guilt. The longer they hold the unhappy soul bound, the graver
are the crimes.[13]

What if some contracted marriage in the old days in the fifth or further
degree; afterwards the Church removed the impediment by establishing that
in such a degree it is licitly possible to marry. They then cohabit for some time.
Is the marriage ratified?

It seems not because in spiritual marriage a choice that was invalid from
the beginning cannot be ratified through subsequent consent.[14] Nonetheless,
I believe that, if they knew the impediment was removed, remained in marital
affection, and were joined carnally, it should be judged as a marriage because
as a rule judgment ought to be in favour of marriage unless an express law is
found against the marriage.[15]

---

[10] RdeP: Extra *de consanguinitate et affinitate*, c. ult. [X 4.14.9].

[11] RdeP: 35 q. 5 "Ad Sedem" [*Decretum* C. 35 q.5 c.2].

[12] RdeP: 35 q. 4 "Consanguinitas" [*Decretum* C. 35 q.4 c.1]; q. 5 c. 1 [*Decretum* C. 35 q.5 c.1].

[13] RdeP: Extra *de consanguinitate*, "Non debet" [X 4.14.8].

[14] RdeP: Extra *de electione*, "Auditis" [X 1.6.29].

[15] RdeP: see above De matrimonio, § "Potest contrahere" [above, Title 2.7], and De sponsalibus, § "Pone quod pueri" [above, Title 1.4] and De impedimento conditionis, the line "Si
vero libera contrahit cum servo ignoranter" [above, Title 1.4].

# Title VII
## Spiritual Relationship

Now that carnal relationship has been sufficiently discussed, we now turn to spiritual relationship, since it is worthier than legal. So we must look at what spiritual relationship is; what its species are; what the law is concerning the marriage of such persons; then what useful matters should be added.

1.    Spiritual relationship is the relationship arising from the conferral of a sacrament or from involvement in it. So, for example, a priest baptizes a child, you receive it from the font (as a godparent), each of you is its spiritual father.[1]

2.    There are three species of spiritual relationship. One is called compaternity, which obtains between the spiritual father of a child and his carnal father, for one co-father is always a spiritual father of the child and the other his carnal father. So the verse:

> One of the co-parents will always be spiritual
> The other carnal, nor does such a rule fail.

The second is called paternity, and this obtains between the one who is received from the font and the one who receives, whether male or female.
The third is called fraternity, which obtains between your spiritual child and your carnal children.

3.    It remains for us to see what the law is concerning the marriage of such people. We will deal first with compaternity. Note that there are two species of compaternity, one direct, that is, when I receive from the sacred font the son of Bertha, a woman, or she receives my child. I can never have this woman as my wife and if I do, the marriage must be dissolved.[2] The other species is called indirect, when one of the spouses, after they have become one flesh, receives the child of others. In this case both spouses are made co-parents of the infant, even the spouse who does not receive the child, since the spouses share the actions of each other.[3]
We shall offer an example to make this clearer. Martin married Bertha and Lothar married Theberga. Afterwards Lothar received the son of Martin and

---

[1] RdeP: 30 q. 1 "Omnes" [*Decretum* C. 30 q.1 c.8]; Extra *de cognatione spirituali*, c. ult. [X 4.11.8].

[2] RdeP: 30 q. 1 c. 1 (in fine) [*Decretum* C. 30 q.1 c.1]; Extra *de cognatione spirituali*, "Veniens" [X 4.11.6].

[3] RdeP: 30 q. 4 "Sciscitatur" [*Decretum* C. 30 q.4 c.1], "Si quis ex uno" [*Decretum* C. 30 q.4 c.3].

Bertha from the sacred font. Then Lothar and Bertha died and there remained Martin and Theberga, who had acquired compaternity by her husband's action. The question is whether Martin is able to contract marriage with Theberga. I reply that there is no way he can.[4] In this way both direct and indirect compaternity impede the contracting of marriage and break off what has already been contracted. This is also gathered from the previously alleged chapters.[5]

4.   It is customary to ask whether someone can marry two co-mothers, one after the other. On this question the following should be held: it depends on whether the commaternity preceded the marriage or followed. If it preceded the marriage, or at least carnal intercourse, one can marry two co-mothers. For example: Mary and Bertha became co-mothers. Afterwards Martin contracted with Bertha. On her death he could contract with Mary even if he had known the first after compaternity, but not before. The reason is because there is no transfer to a preceding union of spirit from a subsequent carnal union.[6]

If, however, commaternity follows the marriage, a distinction is made. If your wife, after being known carnally by you, receives another's child, she whose child was received becomes your co-mother through your wife's action. On your wife's death you cannot have her as your wife. And understand that the same compaternity is acquired by the wife through the husband.[7] If, indeed, some woman raised your wife's child, whom she had by another man, from the sacred font or sponsored the child for confirmation before the bishop, that woman is the co-mother of your wife and not your's. No distinction is made whether intercourse between you and your wife followed or not because no commaternity was acquired in your regard. Therefore, on the death of your wife you can marry such a co-mother of her's. It is the same if your child, whom you fathered through another woman, were received by someone, because no compaternity is acquired for your wife. So in this case, as in the first, someone can marry two co-mothers and a woman two co-fathers.[8]

This distinction concerning marrying two co-mothers can be condensed into four short verses:

> She who raised from the font one born to me or I one of hers
> She is my co-mother, she cannot become my wife.
> If she raised from the font one born of mine not sired by me,
> Her, after the death of mine, I am not thereby barred from having.

---

[4] RdeP: Extra *de cognatione spirituali*, "Martinus Bertham" [X 4.11.4].

[5] [*Decretum* C. 30 q.4 c.1 and 3.]

[6] RdeP: 30 q. 4 "Post uxoris obitum" [*Decretum* C. 30 q.4 c.5].

[7] RdeP: 30 q. 4 "Sciscitatur" [*Decretum* C. 30 q.4 c.1], "Si quis ex uno" [*Decretum* C. 30 q.4 c.3]; Extra *de cognatione spirituali*, "Martinus Bertham [X 4.11.4].

[8] RdeP: 30 q. 4 "Qui spiritualem" [*Decretum* C. 30 q.4 c.4], "Post uxoris" [*Decretum* C. 30 q.4 c.5].

5.   We have dealt with compaternity; now we must look at paternity that obtains between one who receives and one who is received, that is, between a spiritual father and spiritual daughter or between a spiritual mother and a spiritual son. It must be said that marriage is never possible between such people, and if they are joined they must be separated.[9]

What if someone contracted marriage, not with the daughter of the co-father by whom they were made co-fathers, but with another [daughter]? Say that it is proper to refrain from such a marriage; if, however, they have contracted, the marriage stands.[10]

Again, the question arises whether a layman or a cleric in minor orders can contract marriage with her whom he baptized with his own hands. It should be said that he cannot, since she is his spiritual daughter, like her whom he received.[11] But if marriage was contracted between them, are they to be separated? Some say yes.[12] It seems to me that on this matter the Supreme Pontiff is to be consulted since it is a new issue.[13]

6.   Finally, we must examine spiritual fraternity, which obtains between the one received and the carnal sons and daughters of his spiritual father. It should be realized that on this issue there were various opinions at one time and various laws emerged. Some said that children of two co-fathers could never be joined, whether they were born before the compaternity or afterwards. Other laws said that only those born after the compaternity could be joined. Putting all these aside, there is no doubt it must be held that all children of two co-parents, whether born before or after the compaternity, can be legitimately joined in marriage, except the person through whom the compaternity was contracted. That person can never be joined with any of the children of his spiritual father.[14]

Again it is asked if the son of a priest or of another man who baptized a girl can marry her whom his father baptized. Some said yes, but you should hold the contrary because of the new law. Indeed, even if the marriage was contracted it must be broken up.[15]

7.   Finally, for knowledge of all the preceding we must examine through what sacraments spiritual relationship is contracted. Some say that just as there are

---

[9] RdeP: 30 q. 1 "De eo quod interrogasti" [Decretum C. 30 q.1 c.5]; 33 q. 2 "Si quis cum matre spirituali" [Decretum C. 33 q.2 c.17].

[10] RdeP: 30 q. 3 "Illud etiam" [Decretum C. 30 q.3 c.7].

[11] RdeP: 30 q. 1 "Omnes" [Decretum C. 30 q.1 c.8].

[12] RdeP: 30 q. 1 "Omnes" [Decretum C. 30 q.1 c.8], c. "De eo quod interrogasti" [Decretum C. 30 q.1 c.5].

[13] RdeP: Extra de translatione praelatorum, "Inter corporalia" [X 1.7.2].

[14] RdeP: 30 q. 3 "Super quibus" [Decretum C. 30 q.3 c.4], "Pitacium" [Decretum C. 30 q.3 c.2], "Non oportet" [Decretum C. 30 q.3 c.3]; Extra de cognatione spirituali, c. 1 [X 4.11.1], "Tua nos" [X 4.11.7].

[15] RdeP: Extra de cognatione spirituali, c. ult. [X 4.11.8].

seven gifts of the Holy Spirit, so there are seven gifts of baptism, namely, from the first food of the blessed salt right up to confirmation, which is performed by a bishop. In any of them compaternity is contracted so that there can be no marriage between such spiritual relations.[16]

Others say that spiritual relationship is only contracted through three sacraments, namely, catechesis, baptism, and episcopal confirmation.[17]

A third group, with whom I agree, says the same as the second, i.e., that compaternity is contracted by no more than those three. But they differ in this that although compaternity contracted through baptism and confirmation impedes and breaks off a marriage,[18] what is contracted through catechesis is so frail and weak that it barely impedes marriage from being contracted. However, it never breaks off an already contracted marriage.[19] The reason is clear because, since baptism is the door and foundation of all the sacraments,[20] it follows that catechesis is not a sacrament. Again, before baptism one is not a son of the Church, because if he were to die he would perish for eternity, so he was not a spiritual son. Therefore, through it [i.e., catechesis] no or almost no compaternity is contracted.

---

[16] RdeP: 30 q. 1 "Pervenit" (in fine) [*Decretum* C. 30 q.1 c.1].

[17] RdeP: de cons. dist. 4 "In catechismo" [*Decretum, De consec.* D. 4 c.100].

[18] RdeP: 30 q. 1 "Si quis filiastrum" [*Decretum* C. 30 q.1 c.2], "De his qui" [*Decretum* C. 30 q.1 c.6]; and q. 4 "Si quis ex uno" [*Decretum* C. 30 q.4 c.3]; 33 q. 2 "Si quis cum matre spirituali" [*Decretum* C. 33 q.2 c.17]; Extra *de cognatione spirituali* (per totum) [X 4.11].

[19] RdeP: Extra *de cognatione spirituali*, "Contracto" [X 4.11.5].

[20] RdeP: 32 dist. § "Verum" (in fine) [*Decretum* D. 32 d.p.c..6]; Extra *de presbytero non baptizato,* c. 1 et ult. [X 3.43.1 and 3].

# Title VIII
## Legal Relationship

After the treatment of carnal and spiritual relationship, legal relationship must be examined: what it is; what its species are; when and how it might impede marriage.

1.   Legal relationship is a certain proximity arising from adoption. Because in canon law there is little treatment of this matter, we shall add a fuller treatment for the instruction of the simple [i.e., those who are moderately educated but without sophisticated knowledge of the law]. Therefore, we must see what adoption is; what its species are; who can adopt; who can be adopted; what the effect of adoption is.

2.   Adoption is described thus: adoption is the lawful taking in of an outside person as a son or grandson, and so on.
    There are two species of it: one is called adrogation, the other simple adoption. One is adrogated who is independent, that is, who has no father or if he has he was emancipated and passes into the power of the one adrogating. This must be done by the authority of the prince. One is adopted who is in the power of his father and does not pass into the power of the one adopting. This is done through an order of the magistrate.[1] So the verses:

> I adrogate one who is his own, and he is necessarily mine.
> I adopt one who is his father's, and he does not cease being the father's.

3.   A head of household who is independent and who can procreate can adopt, since whoever is unable to procreate, such as a eunuch or one who is frigid, cannot adopt.[2] Again, one who is a minor under twenty cannot adopt, unless a just cause arises, and demonstrated in the following laws.[3] A woman cannot adopt unless it is granted by rescript of the prince in the relief of children who have been lost.[4]
    Anyone can be adopted, male as well as female, as long as he or she is younger than the adoptive father, so that they could be his natural children.[5]

---

[1] RdeP: ff. *de adoptionibus*, Lex 2 [*Digest* 1.7.2] et Lex "Si pater" [*Dig.* 1.7.15].

[2] RdeP: ff. *de adoptionibus*, Lex 2, § "Istud" [*Dig.* 1.7.2,1].

[3] RdeP: ff. eodem titulo, "Si pater" § ult. [*Dig.* 1.7.15, 3].

[4] RdeP: as ff. *de adoptionibus*, "Nam et feminae" [*Dig.* 1.7.21]; C. eodem titulo, "Mulierem" [*Code* 8.47.5].

[5] RdeP: ff. eodem titulo, Lex "Adoptio enim" [*Dig.* 1.7.16].

4.   The effect of adoption is that the one who is adopted is considered as a son in everything so that he would succeed to one [who died] intestate.[6] Again, one who is adrogated and his sons and grandsons, if he has them in his power, pass into the power of the one adrogating. This is not the case for one who is adopted.

Again, there is another difference between one who is adrogated and one who is adopted. A father who adrogates is bound to leave to the adrogated son a fourth part of all he has whether in a will or whether he wishes to emancipate him. But the father who adopts is not bound to leave anything to his adopted son unless he wishes.[7]

5.   At the beginning we saw what legal relationship is. Now we see what its species are and when and how it might impede marriage. Yet it must first be noted that one who is adopted becomes a relation to those alone who are under the power of the adopting father.[8]

6.   There are three species of adoption: one as if in the descending line; another as if coming from the side; a third, which can be called legal affinity. The first, as if in the descending line, obtains between me (the adopting father) and my adopted daughter or granddaughter. The second, as if coming from the side, obtains between my natural son and my adopted daughter. The third, i.e., legal affinity, obtains between me and the wife of my adopted son; likewise between my adopted son and my wife.

Legal relationship in the second species impedes marriage as long as they are in the power of the same father. After it is dissolved by death or the emancipation of the adopted or natural son, it no longer impedes.[9] In the first species, as if in the descending line, and in the third, i.e., legal affinity, it impedes unconditionally[10] at any time, since the adopting father cannot marry his adopted daughter or granddaughter, nor his adopted son's wife, even after emancipation.[11] Likewise, an adopted son, after the death of his adoptive father, cannot contract marriage with his father's wife.[12]

Enough has been said about carnal, spiritual, and legal relationship.

---

[6] RdeP: as C. eodem titulo, Lex paenult. [*Code* 8.47.10].

[7] RdeP: as C. eodem titulo, Lex 1 [*Code* 8.47.1] et Lex paenult. [*Code* 8.47.10].

[8] RdeP: ff. eodem titulo, "Qui in adoptionem" [*Dig.* 1.7.23].

[9] RdeP: Extra *de cognatione legali*, c. 1 [X 4.12.1]; 30 q. 3 "Ita diligere" [*Decretum* C. 30 q.3 c.1], "Post susceptum" [*Decretum* C. 30 q.3 c.5].

[10] Text: *indistincte*

[11] RdeP: ff. *de ritu nuptiarum*, "Nam adoptivus" [*Dig.* 23.2.14]; Inst. *de nuptiis*, § 1, 2, et 3 [*Inst.* 1.10, 1-3].

[12] RdeP: ff. *de ritu nuptiarum*, "Nam adoptivus" [*Dig.* 23.2.14].

# Title IX
## The Impediment of Crime

1.  On account of their enormity there are many crimes such as incest that impede the contracting of marriage.[1] Again, one who killed his wife ought not take another.[2] Again, one who undermines the marriage by receiving his own child from the sacred font, so that he could deprive his spouse of the carnal debt and his wealth.[3] Again, one who kills a priest.[4] Again, one who does solemn penance.[5]

However, although these crimes and perhaps some others impede the contracting of marriage, generally if they are adolescents and there is fear of incontinence, the Church ought to grant them freedom to marry.[6]

2.  Again, note that while there are many crimes that impede the contracting of marriage, as was said above, only three break up a contracted marriage.

The first is if someone commits adultery with a married woman and he or she were to plot in the death of the husband of the adulteress or in the death of the wife of the adulterer so that they might contract marriage after the adultery. In this case they ought not marry and if they did they must be separated.[7]

The second case is if he gives his word to the adulteress that he would marry her after the death of her lawful husband, or after the death of the wife of the adulterer himself.[8]

The third case is when he does not give his word to the adulteress to marry her, but he takes her at the time and contracts marriage with her, since it is a greater thing to take than to give one's word to take.[9]

If none of those cases arises and the adulterer, on the death of his wife or the

---

[1] RdeP: 32 q. 7 "Si quis viduam" [*Decretum* C. 32 q.7 c.20], "Qui dormierit" [*Decretum* C. 32 q.7 c.21], "Concubuisti" [*Decretum* C. 32 q.7 c.23].

[2] RdeP: 33 q. 2 "Admonere" [*Decretum* C. 33 q.2 c.8], "Interfectores" [*Decretum* C. 33 q.2 c.5]. Again, one who abducted another's fiancée, 27 q. 2 "Statutum" [*Decretum* C. 27 q.2 c.34].

[3] RdeP: 30 q. 1 "De eo autem" [*Decretum* C. 30 q.1 c.5].

[4] RdeP: Extra *de paenitentiis et remissionibus*, "Qui presbyterum" [X 5.38.2].

[5] RdeP: 33 q. 2 "De his" [*Decretum* C. 33 q.2 c.12], "Antiqui" [*Decretum* C. 33 q.2 c.19].

[6] RdeP: arg. 33 q. 2 "Antiqui" [*Decretum* C. 33 q.2 c.19], "In adolescentia" [*Decretum* C. 33 q.2 c.14]; Extra *de eo qui cognovit consanguineam uxoris suae*, "Ex litteris" [X 4.13.8].

[7] RdeP: 31 q. 1 "Si quis vivente" [*Decretum* C. 31 q.1 c.5]; Extra *de eo qui duxit in matrimonium quam polluit per adulterium*, "Super hoc" [X 4.7.3], "Significasti" [X 4.7.6], "Veniens" [X 4.7.7].

[8] RdeP: 31 q. 1 "Relatum" [*Decretum* C. 31 q.1 c.4], and in all the preceding chapters.

[9] RdeP: Extra *de eo qui duxit in matrimonium quam polluit per adulterium*, "Cum haberet" [X 4.7.5], "Ex litterarum" [X 4.7. 4].

husband of the adulteress, contracted marriage with her whom he had previously polluted through adultery, the marriage stands, as is said in the same chapters. However, when it was said above that, when the adulterer gave his word to the adulteress or contracted marriage with her while the husband of the adulteress was living or the wife of the adulterer, they ought to be separated, it must be understood to apply when both the adulterer and the adulteress knew of the impediment when they married in that manner. For if one did not know, believing then that the man she married was unmarried, she can be with him after the death of her lawful husband. This is on account of the good faith she had.[10]

Again, note that the first marriage makes the second to be of no avail if, with the first in existence, a second is contracted when the first was true and lawful. If the first was not true but only putative, it offers no impediment to the second marriage.[11] Yet, if the first marriage was contracted before the Church, and the man marries another woman prior to a divorce granted by the Church or contrary to a prohibition by the Church, he sins and must do penance. Nonetheless, the marriage stands.[12]

3.     Suppose a man gives his word to a married woman with whom he has not committed adultery that he would take her after the death of her lawful husband or of his wife if he was married, or he contracts with her in fact with the marriage dissolved after the death of his wife or the husband of the adulteress. Can he marry her, or if he did marry her, must they be separated? It seems that they can marry because the laws alleged above speak of when the adulterer gives his word to the adulteress or contracts with her. This does not apply here.

Solution: It was determined in the new law that, whether he knew her before word was given or marriage was contracted in fact or afterwards, and the lawful wife was still living, by all means they must be separated. Otherwise, if carnal intercourse neither occurred before nor after, although penance must be enjoined on both of them because they seriously went astray, nevertheless the marriage that he contracted with her after the death of his wife must not be broken off.[13]

---

[10] RdeP: Extra *de eo qui duxit in matrimonium*, "Propositum" [X 4.7.1], "Veniens" [X 4.7.7]; Extra *de sponsalibus*, "Cum in Apostolica" [X 4.1.18].

[11] RdeP: Extra *de sponsalibus* "Veniens" [X 4.1.13]; Extra *de matrimonio contracto contra interdictum ecclesiae*, "Ex litteris" (in fine) [X 4.16.2].

[12] RdeP: as was said in the previously alleged decretal: "Ex litteris" (in fine), *de matrimonio contra interdictum ecclesiae contracto* [X 4.16.2].

[13] RdeP: Extra *de eo qui duxit in matrimonium quam polluit per adulterium*, "Si quis uxore" [X 4.7.8].

# Title X
## Dissimilar Religion

1.   The treatment of dissimilar religion follows, that is, when one of those who wish to contract marriage is a catholic and the other a heretic, one a Christian and the other a Jew or a pagan.

In this matter you should make the following distinctions: either a believer contracts marriage with an unbeliever, that is, with a Jew, a pagan, or a heretic; or unbelievers between themselves; or believers between themselves and afterwards one of them falls into heresy.

In the first case there is no marriage. However, a believer can contract an engagement with an unbeliever with the condition that the unbeliever be converted to the faith,[1] as the Lord prohibited in the Old Testament, saying, "You shall not take wives for your sons from the daughters of foreigners, lest they lead them after their gods" (Exod. 34.16).

In the second case, namely, when the spouses are unbelievers such as Jews or Saracens, there is a true marriage. But if one is converted to the faith and the other remains in Judaism or in the error of paganism,[2] if the unbeliever does not wish to cohabit with the believer, or if he wishes to cohabit but not without injury and blasphemy to the name of Christ, or to draw him to infidelity or to another mortal sin, in these three cases the affront to the Creator dissolves the right of marriage for the believer and so the believer can licitly marry [another].[3]

If, however, the unbeliever wishes to cohabit with the believer without any of the aforesaid, the believer, if he wishes to cohabit with the unbeliever, does well because the Apostle admonishes the Corinthians saying, "If a brother has an unbelieving wife [and she consents to dwell with him, let him not put her away]" etc. (1 Cor. 7.12). If he does not want to cohabit with the unbeliever, he must not be forced, but as long as the unbeliever is living the believer cannot marry because the marriage endures.[4]

Although some have made a distinction, saying it is one thing for Jews another for pagan converts because a Jew converted to the faith ought not cohabit with an unbelieving wife who wishes to cohabit, but a converted Saracen or pagan

---

[1] RdeP: 28 q. 1 § "Ex his" (in fine) [*Decretum* C. 28 q.1 d.p.c.14] , "Cave Christiane" [*Decretum* C. 28 q.1 c.15], "Non oportet" [*Decretum* C. 28 q.1 c.16].

[2] Text: *gentilitatis.*

[3] RdeP: Extra *de divortiis*, "Quanto" [X 4.19.7], "Gaudemus" [X 4.19.8].

[4] RdeP: Extra *de divortiis*, "Gaudemus" [X 4.19.8].

can, it seems that today the same judgment applies to both cases.[5]

2.    What if Jews or pagans married blood relatives in accord with their own rites?
Do they remain joined in that way after conversion?

You should say yes because for unbelievers it is a true marriage; they are not
constrained by canonical constitutions; marriages are not dissolved by the sacrament of baptism, but crimes are forgiven.[6] But I understand this to be the case
unless they shall have married within degrees prohibited by divine law (see
Leviticus 18).

3.    What if an unbeliever with many wives at the same time is converted? Will he
keep them all or which of them will he keep?

Say that only the first is the wife and so he can keep her alone. Since indeed
from the beginning one rib was turned into one woman and divine scripture testifies that for this reason a man leaves his father and mother and cleaves to his wife
and they will be two in one flesh (cf. Gen. 2.24); nor did it say three or many but
two; nor did it say he will cleave to wives but wife. It is clear that it was never licit
to have many wives at the same time. It is otherwise if it was granted by divine
revelation through which, just as Jacob was excused from lying, the Israelites from
theft, and Samson from murder, so the Patriarchs and other just men who are read
to have had many wives at the same time were excused from adultery.[7]

It is also clear that if an unbeliever repudiated his lawful wife according to his
own rite, since Truth in the Gospel condemned such a repudiation, as long as she
lives he can never licitly have another even if converted to the faith of Christ, except in the three cases noted above at the beginning of this Title.[8]

4.    But ought a man already converted to the faith be restored to the wife whom
he despoiled unjustly by such a condemned repudiation, if she should seek restoration?

You should say no if she remained an unbeliever up to then because, according to the Apostle, "brother or sister are not bound in such cases" (1 Cor. 7.15).
But if she converted after her husband converted to the faith, aside from the three
reasons noted at the beginning [above Title 10.1] before he may take a lawful wife,
he is compelled to take her back.[9]

This is clearly proven because, if any of the reasons mentioned above at the
beginning should arise[10] the marriage is dissolved immediately as far as duty is

[5] RdeP: Extra de consanguinitate, "De infidelibus" [X 4.14.4]; et Extra eodem titulo, "Interro-
gatum" [Compil. II 3.20.1].

[6] RdeP: Extra de divortiis, "Gaudemus" (in principio) [X 4.19.8]; 26 dist. "Una tantum" [Decre-
tum D. 26 q.4].

[7] RdeP: Extra de divortiis, "Gaudemus, § Quia vero" [X 4.19.8].

[8] [Title 10.1]; RdeP: Extra de divortiis, "Gaudemus, § Qui autem" [X 4.19.8].

[9] RdeP: Extra de divortiis, "Gaudemus, § Qui autem" et § "Quod si conversum" [X 4.19.8].

[10] [Above Title 10.1.]

concerned, but not in reference to its substance, except when at length he contracts marriage with another. Therefore, the Apostle said, "for brother or sister is not bound in such cases" (1 Cor. 7.15), and the canon, "affront to the Creator dissolves the right of marriage for the one left behind." It does not say "it dissolves marriage" but the right, that is, the bond, obligation, or service of marriage.[11] Nonetheless, some feel otherwise, twisting another meaning from the text.

5. In the third case, namely, when believers contract marriage between themselves and afterwards one falls into heresy or the error of unbelief, the one who is abandoned cannot marry regardless of whether carnal intercourse occured or not. And he is bound to be continent, even though in this case affront to the Creator appears greater than in the first case. The reason is because the marriage of believers is ratified and so cannot be dissolved by any situation that might arise. For the sacrament of faith, which once received is never lost, ratifies the sacrament of marriage. The marriage of unbelievers is not ratified and therefore can be legitimately dissolved.[12]

6. What if a catholic man marries a baptized female heretic, or vice versa? Does the marriage stand? It seems that it does not because of dissimilar religion, as was said above at the beginning, and expressly by Ambrose,"Cave Christiane," the verse, "Beware, he says, you do not obtain a pagan, or a Jew, or a foreigner, that is, a heretic, as your wife";[13] and in the chapter, "You ought not mix marriages with heretics."[14] Nonetheless, Huguccio says that, although such a marriage ought not be contracted, once contracted it stands, just as it would hold with an excommunicated person. It is enough if both were initiated by the sacrament of baptism, as in the chapter "Cave Christiane".[15]

But suppose that a Jew, a gentile, or an unbaptized heretic wished to be baptized and he does not find water or a person who would baptize him. It is certain that all his sins are forgiven because he was baptized by the baptism of fire. Can he contract marriage with a Christian woman? Huguccio says that he cannot because baptism is the door to all the sacraments.[16] And he is correct regarding the chapter "Cave", the verse, "It is not enough that she be a Christian, unless both have been initiated into the sacrament of baptism."[17]

[11] RdeP: 28 q. 2 "Si infidelis" [*Decretum* C. 28 q.2 c.2].

[12] RdeP: Extra *de divortiis*, "Quanto" [X 4.19.7].

[13] RdeP: 28 q. 1 [*Decretum* C. 28 q.1 c.15].

[14] [*Decretum* C. 28 q.1 c.16.]

[15] [*Decretum* C. 28 q.1 c.15. Huguccio discusses this question at some length; see Huguccio, *Summa* on Gratian, *Decretum* C. 28 q.1 c.15, ad v. *cave* (Admont, Stifsbibliothek MS 7, fol. 352ra).]

[16] RdeP: 32 dist. § "Verum" [*Decretum* D. 32 d.p.c.6].

[17] [*Decretum* C. 28 q.1 c.15, § 1. See Huguccio, *Summa* on Gratian, *Decretum* C. 28 q.1 c.15, ad v. *cave* (Admont, Stifsbibliothek MS 7, fol. 352rb), "quia baptismus est ianua et primum sacramentorum"–"because baptism is the door and the first of the sacraments."]

# Title XI
## The Impediment of Violence or Fear

1.   Note that by its very nature, even without the constitution of the Church, the impediment of violence or fear excludes matrimonial consent. For consent has no place where fear or force is present, so neither does marriage, which is contracted through consent alone.[1] But because between force and force there is a great difference and between fear and fear,[2] we must look at what force or coercion is and what fear is; what violence excuses and what fear excuses.

2.   Force is the impulse of a greater thing that cannot be repelled.[3] Fear is mental trepidation at a present or future danger, as is read in the same law.[4]

3.   However, that you might know what force or fear excuses, note that some coercion or force is slight, another violent. Slight force does not exclude marital consent; violent force excludes consent.[5] It is clear what violent coercion is, for example, when one is captured or dragged, lead away unwillingly, or bound.[6]
   Again, some fear falls on a steadfast man, another does not. What falls on a steadfast man excuses and excludes marital consent.[7] However, what would be the fear that would fall on a steadfast man and excuse? Say that it would be fear of death and bodily torture.[8] Again, fear of sexual violation[9] and enslavement.[10] You might group these four types of fear in two verses:

> For example these fears can excuse, because you do not know,
> Of being sexually violated, or of status, of blows, and of death.

---

[1] RdeP: 27 q. 2 "Sufficiat" [*Decretum* C. 27 q.2 c.2]; Extra *de sponsalibus*, "Cum locum" [X 4.1.14].

[2] RdeP: Extra *de sponsalibus*, "De muliere" [X 4.1.6].

[3] RdeP: ff *quod metus causa*, Lex 1, § ult. [*Dig.* 4.2.2].

[4] [*Dig.* 4.2.1.]

[5] RdeP: arg. dist. 50 "Presbyteros" [*Decretum* D. 50 c.32]; Extra *de sponsalibus*, "Veniens" (2) [X 4.1.15]; 31 q. 2 c. 1 et 2 [*Decretum* C. 31 q.2 c.1-2].

[6] RdeP: Extra *De his quae vi metusve causa fiunt*, "Sacris" [X 1.40.5].

[7] RdeP: Extra *de his quae vi metusve causa*, "Perlatum" [X 1.40.1], "Ad audientiam" [X 1.40. 4], "Sacris" [X 1.40.5]; Extra *de sponsalibus*, "Veniens" (2) [X 4.1.15].

[8] RdeP: Extra *de his quae vi metusve causa fiunt*, "Cum dilectus filius" [X 1.40.6].

[9] Text: *stupri*

[10] RdeP: ff. eodem titulo, "Nec timorem" [*Dig.* 4.2.7], "Isti quidem" § 1, 2, et 3 [*Dig.* 4.2.8].

Again, note that such fear might fall on one and would not be said to fall on another because it is not likely that men of distinguished worth would have been afraid in the city or that a king should fear a small army.[11] Nevertheless, if he has the clearest proofs of this fear, the presumption against him is removed, as is said in the same place. In this way a judge will judge what the quality of the fear is according to the differences of persons and places, and will judge the marriage to be something or nothing.

4.   Again, note that whatever be the fear or violence in contracting a marriage, if the woman, who alleges fear, remained for a year and a half with her husband or consented to carnal intercourse, she ought not be heard afterwards if she alleges fear or violence.[12]

---

[11] RdeP: ff. *quod metus causa*, "Non est verisimile" [*Dig.* 4.2.23]; 31 q. 2 "Lotharius" [*Decretum* C. 31 q.2 c.4].

[12] RdeP: Extra *de sponsalibus*, "Ad id quod" [X 4.1.21]; Extra *qui matrimonium accusare possunt*, "Insuper adiecisti" [X 4.18.4]; Extra *de eo qui duxit in matrimonium quam polluit per adulterium*, "Significavit" [X 4.7.2].

# Title XII
# The Impediment of Orders

Now the impediment of orders must be discussed. Note that clerics in minor orders, unless they are monks, or regular canons, or those in another religious order that professes continence, can licitly marry.[1] If, however, someone is established in holy orders, namely a priest, deacon, or subdeacon, he cannot marry and if he should have contracted marriage it will be dissolved.[2]

[1] RdeP: D. 32.3], "Seriatim" [*Decretum* D. 32 c.14]; 28 dist. "De his" [*Decretum* D. 28 c.5]; Extra *de clericis coniugatis*, c. 1, 2, et 3 [X 3.3.1-3].

[2] RdeP: dist. 32 "Si quis eorum" [*Decretum* D. 32 c.7], "Lectores" [*Decretum* D. 32 c.8], "Erubescant" [*Decretum* D. 32 c.11], "Placuit" [*Decretum* D. 32 c.13]; Extra *qui clerici vel voventes matrimonium contrahere possunt*, c. 1 et 2 [X 4.6.1-2]. For useful matter on this see *Summa de paenitentia*, in titulo De votis, § "Item quid si maritus" [Raymond of Penyafort, *Summa de paenitentia* 1.8.15 (ed. Ochoa and Díez, col. 358)].

# Title XIII
## The Impediment of Bond

The treatment of the impediment of bond[1] follows, that is, when one is bound to another spouse or fiancé(e). This impediment was always operative even before anything was established by the Church in the matter. A man bound to a wife never can or could take another, nor was it ever permitted. If one did this he committed adultery, except one to whom there was divine revelation through the instigation of the Holy Spirit, such as to the patriarchs.[2]

1. Since some are bound by engagements, some by marriages, we look at what the law is in both cases, and first, engagements.

It is to be noted that if someone contracts an engagement through words in the future tense, he ought not contract with another woman, nor the woman with another man. If he has contracted only an engagement likewise through words in the future tense, he must dismiss the second and return to the first. But if he contracted with the second through words in the present tense, or through words in the future tense followed by carnal intercourse, he must remain with the second and do penance for his bad faith.[3] What little is said here on this matter will be found more fully treated above, [Title 1.6].[4]

2. If a man is bound to his wife in marriage, that is, because they contracted through words in the present tense, if they have not yet been made one flesh by carnal union, one can transfer to religious life, even if the other objects, and the one remaining can contract with another.[5] However, if carnal union between them followed, it is never permitted for the husband to dismiss his wife or for the wife to dismiss her husband, except on account of fornication. Then he can dismiss her without being able to take another, and if he has dismissed her he should be reconciled to his wife or remain without a wife. If he takes another, he commits adultery.[6]

[1] Text: *ligatio*

[2] RdeP: Extra *de divortiis*, "Gaudemus, § 1" [X 4.19.8], and above, [Title 10.2] De dispari cultu, § "Quid si infidelis".

[3] RdeP: Extra *de sponsa duorum*, c. 1 [X 4.4.1]; Extra *de sponsalibus*, "Sicut ex litteris" [X 4.1.22].

[4] RdeP: in titulo De sponsalibus, § ult.

[5] RdeP: Extra *de conversione coniugatorum*, "Verum" [X 3.32.2], "Ex publico" [X 3.32.7]; Extra *de sponsa duorum*, "Licet praeter solitum" [X 4.4.3].

[6] RdeP: 32 q. 7 c. 1, 2, et 3 [*Decretum* C. 32.7.1-3].

3.    Suppose a wife believes her husband is dead and she contracts with another. Say that as long as she believes it and he does not return she is excused from adultery and fornication on account of the ignorance of fact. If she had children with the second, they are judged to be legitimate; but as soon as the first returns she must leave the second and return to the first. If she does not do this, she is to be judged an adulteress.[7]

But what if he does not return and, nevertheless, she believes he is alive; what should she do? She should not demand the debt from the [second] husband, but pay if he demands.[8]

4.    Again, suppose the husband has gone in the army against the Saracens or to a faraway region and he does not return, nor is it known whether he is living or dead. What should his wife do?

Say that regardless of her youth she cannot contract until she is certain of the death of her husband.[9] But how will that be resolved? I reply: by an oath of one under whom he fought or even of friends who knew well of his death. She can marry immediately after such an oath.[10]

[7] RdeP: 34 q. 2 "Cum per bellicam" [*Decretum* C. 34.2.1], "Cum in captivitate" [Gratian C. 34.2.2], "Si virgo" [*Decretum* C. 34.2.5].

[8] RdeP: Extra *de secundis nuptiis*, "Dominus ac Redemptor" [X 4.21.2].

[9] RdeP: Extra *de sponsalibus*, "In praesentia" [X 4.1.19].

[10] RdeP: Extra *de secundis nuptiis*, "Super illa" [X 4.21.4].

# Title XIV
## The Justice of the Public Good

1. After discussing the impediment of bond, we should examine the justice of the public good. This impediment was introduced by the Church because of its honesty. At one time there were two species of it, one that was contracted from second marriages, and this is removed from discussion today;[1] the other is contracted from engagements. For example, if someone was engaged to a girl of seven years or beyond, even though he did not know her, nonetheless, none of his blood relations can have her as a wife.[2] I said "of seven years" because if the engagement was contracted before the seventh year, it is judged to be of no significance, nor does it present any impediment unless, after the seventh year, the one who contracted beforehand approved of the engagement.[3]

2. What if engagements do not stand because they were not contracted according to law but simply as a matter of fact? For example, a man was engaged to a blood relative, or a monk, or a cleric in holy orders, or one who is frigid, or bewitched with a perpetual bewitching, or a eunuch as a matter of fact engages a woman. Do such engagements, which come to naught, present an impediment to blood relatives such that they would not be able to contract with such fiancées as a matter of fact, or if they did contract the marriage would not hold?

On this matter Huguccio says (and many agree with him) that of course through such situations an impediment for blood relatives is formed.[4]

It seems to me that the aforesaid opinion rests on the law. However, not because of affinity, which is only contracted through carnal union, but is on account of the justice of the public good, which is contracted through engagements or through words in the present tense or the future tense, whether by law or only contracted as a matter of fact. An exception is the case mentioned above when,

---

[1] RdeP: Extra *de consanguinitate et affinitate*, "Non debet" [X 4.14.8].

[2] RdeP: Extra *de sponsalibus*, c. 1 [X 4.1.1], "Iuvenis" [X 4.1. 3], "Ad audientiam" [X 4.1. 4]; Extra *de desponsatione impuberum*, "Continebatur, § ult." [X 4.2.6].

[3] RdeP: Extra *de desponsatione impuberum*, "Litteras" [X 4.2.4], "Accesit" [X 4.2.5]. And see above De sponsalibus, § "Pone quod pueri" [Title 1.4].

[4] RdeP: On the first case you expressly have: Extra *de sponsalibus*, "Ad audientiam" [X 4.1.4]. For all the cases it seems you have expressly: 27 q. 2 "Si quis uxorem desponsaverit" [*Decretum* C. q.27 q.2 c.14], "Quidam desponsaverit" [*Decretum* C. 27 q.2 c.31]. [On these two texts of Gratian see Huguccio, *Summa* on Gratian, *Decretum* C. 27 q.2 c.14 and c. 31 (Admont, Stifsbibliothek ms. 7, fols. 342vb and 345vb).]

for instance, a boy or girl contracts an engagement before the seventh year, in the same place, at the beginning [see Title 14.1]. This is perhaps a special case because in such people there is a defect both of mind and body.

# Title XV
## Affinity

The justice of the public good has been spoken of and since some have viewed it as affinity because of a certain similarity, we shall treat of affinity next. We must look at: what affinity is; how many kinds of affinity there are; how affinity is contracted; to what degree would marriage be prohibited.

1.   Affinity is a relationship between persons arising from carnal union, lacking any blood relationship. I said "from carnal union" because affinity is contracted through the union of fornication as well as through lawful union.[1]

2.   Of old there were three kinds of affinity, but today only the first is extant, the second and third are no longer relevant.[2]
     The first kind of affinity is contracted from a person added to consanguinity through carnal union according to the rule that says: a person added to a person through carnal propagation changes the degree and not the kind of relationship, and a person added to a person through carnal union changes the kind of relationship but not the degree. So the verse:

Marriage changes the kind, but the procreated change the degree.

To understand this better we offer an example: I and my sister are one in consanguinity. My sister takes a husband or she has a lover P. Thus P is a person added to my consanguine relation through carnal union. It changes the kind of contact but not the degree because just as my sister is my consanguine relation in the first degree, so P is my affine relation in the first degree. And what was said of my sister you should understand of any of my male or female blood relations, because all the husbands of my female blood relatives are my affine relations in the first kind of affinity and in the degrees in which their wives are related to me. If a woman is related to me in the second degree of consanguinity, her husband is related to me in the first kind of affinity and in the second degree. If she is related to me in the third degree, her husband is related to me in the first kind of affinity and in the third degree, and so for the other degrees, since degrees are computed between affine relations in respect of consanguinity alone.[3]

---

[1] RdeP: 35 q. 3 "Nec eam" [*Decretum* C. 35 q.3 c.10]; Extra *de eo qui cognovit consanguineam uxoris suae*, "Discretionem" [X 4.13.6], "Tuae fraternitatis" [X 4.13.10].

[2] RdeP: Extra *de consanguinitate*, "Non debet" [X 4.14.8].

[3] RdeP: 35 q. 5 "Porro" [*Decretum* C. 35 q.5 c.3].

All that was said of the husbands of my female blood relations you should
understand of the wives of my male blood relatives because they are all my affine
relatives in the first kind of affinity, and in the degrees in which their husbands are
my blood relations. I likewise am their relation through affinity in the same kind
and the same degrees.

Again, all the male blood relations of my wife are my affine relations in the
first kind of affinity, and in the same degrees in which they are blood relations of
my wife. And all my male blood relations in the same way are affine relations of
my wife in the first kind of affinity and in the same degrees in which they are my
male blood relations.[4]

Of old this first kind of affinity implied prohibition to the seventh degree;
today up to the fourth degree, just like consanguinity itself.[5]

3.   In sum, then, it must not be overlooked that degrees are said to be in affinity
and they are computed with regard to consanguinity alone. So when it is a question of the degree of relationship in regard to the affinity of persons recourse must
be had to the person through whom the affinity arose. It must be asked how many
degrees he is distant from the person in question in accord with the rule noted
above [Title 6] where it was shown how degrees are to be computed.[6] By whatever
degree they are distant in consanguinity, by that they are distant in affinity.

Again, note that if a person, who is an affine relation through addition to you,
procreates a child and procreates it from your [male] consanguine relation, the
child is your relation by consanguinity, not affinity. But if she procreates a child
from one unrelated and not from a consanguine relation the child will have no
relation to you. I said "through addition to you" because if someone is your affine
relation through the addition of you, that is, you would be added to his consanguine line, if he procreates a child, the child will be related to you by affinity, just
as its parent, in the same kind but in another degree.

4.   Again, note that even though the consanguine relation through whom the affinity was contracted should die, the surviving person remains related by affinity.[7]

Again, affinity is contracted not only through marital intercourse but also
through fornication as long as it occurs according to the order of nature. If, indeed, a man pollutes a woman outside of that order, that is, outside of or around
the proper vessel, his blood relatives are not impeded from marrying this woman,
although such pollution is criminal and damnable unless done with marital con-

---

[4] RdeP: This is all proven: Extra *de consanguinitate*, "Quod super his" [X 4.14.5]; 35 q. 2 "Sane"
[*Decretum* C. 35 q.2 c.14].

[5] RdeP: 35 q. 2 "De affinitate" [*Decretum* C. 35.2.1], "Nullum" [*Decretum* 35 q.2 c. 7], "Ae-
qualiter" [*Decretum* C. 35 q.2 c.13]; Extra *de consanguinitate et affinitate*, "Quod super his" [X 4.14.5],
"Non debet" [X 4.14.8].

[6] RdeP: in titulo *de consanguinitate*.

[7] RdeP: 35 q. 10 "Fraternitatis" [*Decretum* C. 35 q.10 c.1].

sent.[8] The reason for saying this is because such pollution neither makes for mixing of blood nor unity of the flesh through which affinity is contracted.[9]

5.    What if he invaded the cloister of modesty but nonetheless did not reach consummation of the act? I believe what was just said above [is the reply] for the same reason.

---

[8] RdeP: 35 q. 3 "Extraordinaria" [*Decretum* C. 35 q.3 c.11]; Extra *de eo qui cognovit consanguineam uxoris suae*, "Fraternitati tuae" [X 4.13.7].

[9] RdeP: 35 q. 10 "Fraternitatis" [*Decretum* C. 35 q.10 c.1].

# Title XVI
## The Impossibility of Intercourse

Among the impediments of marriage, the impossibility of intercourse holds a most important place because it impedes marriage by its very nature, rather than by the constitution of the Church. For, since every marriage comes about either by reason of having offspring or because of incontinence, the impossibility of intercourse removes both reasons. But because not every impossibility of intercourse excludes marital consent, to clarify more fully what ought to be done by law in this matter, we must examine: what the impossibility of intercourse is; what its species are; what impossibility of intercourse impedes matrimony and what does not; how and when divorce ought to occur when the impossibility of intercourse is alleged.

1.   Impossibility of intercourse is a defect[1] of spirit or body or both that impedes one from carnally uniting with another.

There are many species: one is natural impotence such as frigidity in a man, constriction in a woman, failure of age in a child; another is accidental, such as castration, bewitchment,[2] which comes about through spells[3] that are called casting lots or charms.[4] Again, natural impotence is temporary or perpetual.

Natural and temporary impotence that is in a child impedes marriage, which cannot be contracted as long as it is in the child.[5]

Natural impotence in a frigid man, which is perpetual, impedes the contracting of marriage and breaks off what is already contracted.[6]

2.   In regard to constriction, which is in women on account of which they are not suited to male embraces, it is to be held that, although it is by nature, if she can be aided by the benefit of medicine or through assiduous use with a man of suitable size, it does not impede marriage.[7] A consequence of this is that if, because of constriction she separates from a first man, who is unable to know her, and

---

[1] Text: *vitium*

[2] Text: *maleficium*

[3] Text: *maleficia*

[4] Text: *facturae*. [I would like to thank Prof. Richard Kieckhefer of Northwestern University for helpful suggestions for the translation of words relating to bewitchment.]

[5] RdeP: 30 q. 2 c.1 [*Decretum* C. 30 q.2 c.1]; Extra *de frigidis et maleficiatis*, "Quod Sedem [X 4.15.2].

[6] RdeP: 33 q. 1 c.1 et 2 [*Decretum* C. 33 q.1 c.1-2]; Extra *de frigidis et maleficiatis*, "Laudabilem" [X 4.15.5].

[7] RdeP: Extra *de frigidis et maleficiatis*, "Ex litteris" [X 4.15.3].

through the use of another with whom she joins afterwards she becomes suited to the first, she must be separated from the second and returned to the first.[8] If, though, it is constriction that cannot be helped without bodily danger to her, it impedes marriage from being contracted and breaks off one already contracted, just like frigidity itself.[9]

3. We have considered natural impotence; now we should examine accidental impotence, and first, castration, namely when one has his genitals cut off. In this it must be firmly held that such men, who are unsuited to pay the debt, cannot contract marriage just as children cannot,[10] and if they did contract they must be separated because there is no marriage. If the marriage preceded the castration, the marriage is not undone even though the husband becomes unsuited to pay the debt to his wife.[11]

What has been said of castration that comes later, which does not undo a marriage must be understood of any impediment because if it comes later it does not invalidate a marriage already legitimately contracted.

The same is to be understood of the impossibility of intercourse that arises through bewitchment; if it came after the marriage it does not break it up. If it precedes, a distinction is made: either the bewitchment is temporary or perpetual. If it is temporary, no impediment is offered to marriage. If it is perpetual, it impedes the contracting of marriage and breaks off one already contracted.[12]

If you should ask how it is known whether the bewitchment is temporary or perpetual, I respond: from the beginning any bewitchment is presumed to be temporary because every man is presumed to be capable of intercourse. If the impediment lasts after cohabiting for three years and attempting carnal union, the bewitchment is presumed to be perpetual.

Yet some of the learned hold the opposite, saying that no bewitchment separates a marriage already contracted, alluding to the custom of the Roman Church which is accustomed to judge in similar cases that those whom husbands cannot have as wives they should have as sisters.[13] They even say that the chapter "Si per sortiarias"[14] does not hold; but their opinion is to be totally rejected as harsh and too onerous because it would offer material for homicide if a man were to stay with his wife and was not able to know her, but he was potent and suited to another woman. Again, it seems that it can be shown rationally that they are of a wrong opinion since every marriage is entered into by reason of incontinence or

---

[8] RdeP: Extra *de impotentia coeundi*, "Fraternitatis" [X 4.15.6].

[9] RdeP: as in the previously alleged decretals: "Ex litteris" [X 4.15.3], "Fraternitatis" [X 4.15.6].

[10] RdeP: Extra *de frigidis et maleficiatis*, "Quod Sedem" [X 4.15.2].

[11] RdeP: 32 q. 7 "Illi qui" [*Decretum* C. 32 q.7 c.25]; Extra *ut lite non contestata*, "Quoniam frequenter" [X 2.6.5].

[12] RdeP: 33 q. 1 "Si per sortiarias" [*Decretum* C. 33 q.1 c.4].

[13] RdeP: Extra *de frigidis et maleficiatis*, "Consultationi" [X 4.15.4].

[14] [*Decretum* C. 33 q.1 c.4.]

for offspring. But these reasons fail when intercourse is impeded by bewitchment. Therefore, with those reasons in default, there is no marriage.

4. Finally, how and when separation ought to be effected when the impossibility of intercourse is alleged must be examined. To this some wise men have said that if it is alleged that the impossibility is because of the frigidity of a man, or castration, or the constriction of a woman, divorce can be proclaimed since these impediments can be immediately apparent, at least by inspection of the body.[15] But if they are said to be impotent through bewitchment they ought not to be separated for three years.[16] Those who say this seem indeed reasonably to be persuaded, but a decretal opposes them, although there is an argument in their favour in the same decretal.[17] Consequently, it seems to me that it must be said that, unless by the clearest signs and proofs it is certain that they are frigid or constricted so that it is not possible for them to be helped through human aid, they are not to be separated before three years.[18]

Again, note that this is the difference between the frigid and the bewitched. The frigid is unable to know any woman or be moved to desire intercourse, but the bewitched is able to know women other than her with whom he has been bewitched. Therefore, when divorce is proclaimed by reason of frigidity permission is not granted the man to marry another and if he should marry, the second marriage is to be separated and the first restored since it seems the Church was deceived.[19] It is the same if there is separation on account of the woman's constriction, if she marries another.[20] It is otherwise if the spouses are separated because of bewitchment since, even though the man should marry another, he is not returned to the first.[21]

5. Now it must be seen how divorce is to be effected if both parties proceed to judgment and make a defence (or only one of them), and both confess that they are unable to unite carnally.

Indeed, unless the impediment for which they qualify to be separated is immediately evident, as was said, they must be commanded to cohabit again, giving themselves to intercourse in good faith. If, after cohabiting for three years, they are unable to become one flesh, then they ought to swear by the seventh hand[22]

---

[15] RdeP: and they have in their favour Extra *de frigidis et maleficiatis*, c. 1 [X 4.15.1].

[16] RdeP: as in Auth. *de nuptiis*, § "Per occasionem" (*Novels* 22.6).

[17] RdeP: Extra *de frigidis et maleficiatis*, "Laudabilem" [X 4.15.5].

[18] RdeP: as in the previously alleged decretal: "Laudabilem" [X 4.15.5], et in Auth. *de nuptiis*, § "Per occasionem" (*Novels* 22.6). Arg. Extra *de frigidis et maleficiatis*, "Fraternitatis" [X 4.15.6].

[19] RdeP: 33 q. 1 "De his requisisti" [*Decretum* C. 33 q.1 c.2].

[20] RdeP: Extra *de frigidis et maleficiatis*, "Fraternitatis" [X 4.15.6].

[21] RdeP: 33 q. 1 "Si per sortiarias" [*Decretum* C. 33 q.1 c.4].

[22] [See Gratian, *Decretum* C. 33 q.1 c.2. The expression "the seventh hand" refers to an apparently Germanic custom whereby the oaths of the couple were certified by the oaths of seven close acquaintances. The text originated with Burchard of Worms, *Decretum* 9.44 (PL 140.822).

of relatives or of good neighbours before a judge who is familiar with the case. However, the man ought to swear that he gave himself to intercourse in good faith and without fraud to know her and was unable to accomplish it. The woman will swear that it was not her fault (nor did she use fraud) that her husband did not know her but she was not known by him.

The witnesses[23] will swear that they believe them to have sworn the truth.[24] Witnesses or compurgators ought to know their life and manner of living and be unwilling to commit perjury.[25] After these oaths, if they are separated for frigidity, the woman is given permission to marry, but not the man.[26] If on account of the woman's constriction, the man is given permission to marry, but not the woman.[27] If afterwards he to whom permission was denied contracted, the second marriage is to be dissolved and the first re-established. If they were separated because of bewitchment, both are granted permission to marry.[28]

However, if the woman objects saying that the man cannot know her and the man says he can and he confirmed with an oath that he did know her, the oath of the man must stand because he is the head of the woman,[29] unless the woman wishes to respond against him because she would call him a liar and shows through bodily inspection that she is a virgin.[30] Then the woman's proof must stand and because of such a proof they can be separated.

If, however, the husband calls for a judgment and says he could not know his wife and she says she was known by him, if other proofs do not favour the man, he must not be believed in this case even though he is called the head of the woman. The reason is because he initiated the case and if he does not prove what he asserted the woman ought to be cleared of her husband's charge,[31] since she is the defendant even if she offers no testimony; and because if the word of the man were to be believed, many would not fear to incur perjury so that they could be separated from their wives. Yes, even if both spouses were to confess against the

---

See L. Machielson, "Les spurii de s. Grégoire le Grand en matière matrimoniale, dans les collections canoniques jusqu'au *Décret* de Gratien," *Sacris Erudiri* 14 (1963): 252-254. For the treatment of impotence cases by ecclesiastical courts see Jacqueline Murray, "On the origins and role of 'wise women' in causes for annulment on grounds of male impotence," *Journal of Medieval History* 16 (1990): 235-249.]

[23] Text: *sacramentales*

[24] RdeP: arg. Extra *de purgatione canonica*, "Quotiens" [X 5.34.5].

[25] RdeP: Extra *de purgatione canonica*, "Inter sollicitudines" [X 5.34.10].

[26] RdeP: 33 q. 1 "Requisisti" [*Decretum* C. 33 q.1 c.2].

[27] RdeP: Extra *de frigidis et maleficiatis*, "Fraternitatis" [X 4.15.6].

[28] RdeP: 33 q. 1 "Si per sortiarias" [*Decretum* C. 33 q.1 c.4].

[29] RdeP: 33 q. 1 "Si quis accepit" [*Decretum* C. 33 q.1 c.3]; Extra *de desponsatione impuberum*, "Continebatur" [X 4.2.6].

[30] RdeP: arg. 27 q. 1 "Nec aliqua" [*Decretum* C. 27 q.1 c.4]; and expressly at: Extra *de probationibus*, "Proposuisti" [X 2.19.4].

[31] RdeP: 6 q. 4 "Actor" [*Decretum* C. 6 q.4 c.7]; Extra *de causa possessionis et proprietatis*, "Cum Ecclesia" [X 2.12.3]; Extra *de iureiurando*, c. ult. [X 2.24.36].

marriage, it must not for this reason be dissolved by the Church,[32] both because some would wish to conspire between themselves against the marriage if they believed their confession were to stand, and because of the presumption in favour of the marriage.[33]

6. Therefore, that the end correspond with the beginning and the middle with both extremes, it should be known that all the impediments enumerated above, when they arise before the marriage is contracted and respecting the distinctions dealt with for each impediment, impede marriage from being contracted and break off what is already contracted. But if they follow afterwards they neither impede nor break off the marriage.

7. In sum, it must be noted that the impediments explained above are relevant when those who ought to contract marriage are both believers. But if they are both unbelievers and are joined legitimately according to their own rite, if they are converted to the faith, even though they are related by blood or affinity in the second or third degree, they ought not to be separated on that account.[34] But if one is a believer and the other an unbeliever, they cannot contract.[35]

---

[32] RdeP: as above eodem, § "Nunc videndum" [Title 16.5].

[33] RdeP: Extra *de eo qui cognovit consanguineam uxoris*, "Super eo" [X 4.13.5]; Extra *de sententia et re iudicata*, c. ult. [X 2.27.26].

[34] RdeP: Extra *de divortiis*, "Gaudemus" (in principio) [X 4.19.8], "Is qui Ecclesiam" [X 4.19.9].

[35] RdeP: see above De dispari cultu [above, Title 10].

# Title XVII
## The Impediment of Feast Days

After dealing with the impediments to marriage that impede the contracting of marriage and break off what is already contracted, we must follow up with an examination of those that impede the contracting of marriage but do not break off one already contracted. These are feast days, and the prohibition of the Church.

1.  In the time of feast days engagements can be contracted and even marriage, which is contracted through consent alone. But the handing over of the wife, nuptial solemnities, and carnal union are prohibited.[1]

2.  Again, the times of feast days are: from the Advent of the Lord to the octave of the Epiphany, from Septuagesima to the octave of Easter, the three weeks before the feast of Blessed John the Baptist.[2] In regard to these three weeks, nevertheless, at one time there were diverse opinions about when they should begin. But today it is established that they begin three days before the Ascension of the Lord and stretch to the octave of Pentecost.[3]

---

[1] RdeP: Extra *de matrimonio contracto contra interdictum Ecclesiae,* per totum [X 4.16]; 33 q. 4 "Non oportet" and the three following chapters [*Decretum* C. 33 q.4 c.8-11].

[2] RdeP: 33 q. 4 "Non oportet a Septuagesima" [*Decretum* C. 33 q.4 c.10].

[3] RdeP: Extra *de feriis,* "Capellanus" [X 2.9.4].

# Title XVIII
## Marriage Contracted against the Prohibition of the Church

1.  The treatment of the prohibition of the Church follows, namely, when someone is prohibited from contracting with a woman because perhaps it is said she is his blood relation, or related by affinity, or another's fiancée, or perhaps on account of something else.

On this issue different men have written different things, which for now are better passed over in silence than mentioned. But without doubt it must be held that those whose marriage is forbidden ought not contract but if they do contract, unless another perpetual impediment impedes, they can remain together and are not to be separated except for a time so they might do penance for holding the command of the Church in contempt, as is expressly read.[1] If, indeed, some decrees are found that say those joined in such a way must be separated, the text must be explained to show they must be separated for a time, as has been said. The three aforementioned decretals expressly say this.

2.  To avoid various dangers regarding marriage, it was laid down in the general council that, whenever marriages were to be contracted in churches they are to be announced publicly by priests, for a suitable time frame so that within it whoever wishes and is able might bring forward a legitimate impediment. The priests should also themselves investigate whether any impediment stands in the way. If a probable opinion appears against contracting the union, the contract is expressly forbidden until what is to be done about it is established by means of clear documents.

"If, however, a parish priest or any regular who presumed to be present at them contemns to prohibit such unions, he shall be suspended from his office for three years. He must be more severely punished if the quality of the fault requires it. An appropriate penance should be enjoined on those who would presume to be joined in that way, even within a permissible degree. If someone should maliciously offer an impediment as an objection to impede a lawful union, beyond the penance they must do for the sin they must not escape the canonical punishment,." This is all proven.[2]

This is enough said about the impediments to marriage.

---

· [1] RdeP: Extra *de matrimonio contracto contra interdictum Ecclesiae*, per totum [X 4.16].

[2] RdeP: Extra *de clandestina desponsatione*, "Cum inhibitio" (circa principium), et § "Sane" et § "Si quis autem" [X 4.3.3].

# Title XIX
## How and When a Woman Can Bring Suit against Someone as Being Her Husband, or Seek the Restoration of a Husband If She Was Despoiled, or Conversely

After discussing the impediments to marriage—what they are, their nature, and what the law is for each impediment—it is useful to touch in a summary way on how to proceed in matrimonial cases so that one might receive a penitential judgment as to what is one's own.

Note that in this regard sometimes it is a question of preserving a marriage, sometimes a question of dissolving a marriage. Again, if to dissolve, either the divorce is proclaimed completely so that both of them can contract marriage [again], or one alone, as was said [above, Title 16],[1] or it is proclaimed partially, namely, in reference to mutual service of the carnal debt or of cohabitation, so that neither is permitted to contract [again]. This occurs in those who are separated on account of adultery, or fornication, or by reason of religious life. We should look in an orderly way at how one is to act in each of these. But since neither union nor separation is to be done unless through certain accusers and witnesses, we will show: who can bring an accusation against the marriage or to testify in a matrimonial case; and what children are judged to be legitimate; finally, we shall add a treatment of dowry, which is an accessory to the marriage.

1. If a woman brings suit against someone as being her husband (or conversely), it must be seen whether the plaintiff wishes to intend a petitory or possessory judgment. That is, whether the woman says someone is her husband because he married her and she petitions that he be judged her husband, which is to act as a claimant[2] as if she were acting in regard to property; or she petitions that he be restored to her because she was unjustly dismissed by him, who she says contracted marriage with her. This is to act as a possessor[3] since she seeks the possession of her husband to be judged in her favour from which possession she says she was unjustly expelled. These different petitions must be dealt with.

If a woman acts as a claimant, that is, she asks for a man saying he was her husband, and he denies and defends against her saying "you cannot be my wife

---

[1] RdeP: in titulo *De impotentia coeundi.*

[2] Text: *petitorio*

[3] Text: *possessorio*

because you are my blood relation or relation by affinity" or he objects with some other legitimate impediment, the husband's defence will be treated first before the petition of the wife since, if the husband's defence is proved, the wife's principal claim is defeated and the man must be absolved from her accusation.[4]

If she acts as possessor, namely seeking that her husband be restored to her, although the husband says "you cannot be my wife because there is consanguinity between us" or if he claims some other impediment or another crime, restoration ought to be made to the woman before the man's defence is known.[5]

However, when it was said that the woman is to be restored without any defence, this does not hold in certain cases.

The first is if public fornication is claimed against the woman. Then restoration ought not be made if this were proved, or she herself confesses, or it is so notorious that it cannot be hidden by any evasion, unless she replies and proves the man has committed adultery. Then he should be restored to her, even though she fornicated publicly.[6]

Another case is if consanguinity that is prohibited by divine law is claimed and he is prepared to prove this immediately. For in this case, although restoration is made in other matters, yet no restoration is made in regard to carnal union.[7]

A third case is if a defence is raised concerning a matter already decided from which no appeal was made. Then restoration must not be made unless that judgment is first recognized.[8]

A fourth case is one in which a man seeking restoration ought not be restored, namely when his ferocity is such that no sufficient security can be provided to the fearful woman, or because he pursues his wife with deadly hatred.[9]

In all other cases I believe the woman seeking restoration of her husband must receive restoration, and vice versa, as long as she proves she was in possession and deprived of the husband without legal directive; and that she ought to prove these two matters is proven.[10] If she deprives herself of her own right, namely, by leaving her husband on her own authority and without fault of her husband, then, although she seeks restoration, she is not to be heard because then it is not she but rather her husband who is said to be despoiled.[11]

---

[4] RdeP: , Extra *de ordine cognitionum*, c. 1 [X 2.10.1].

[5] RdeP: Extra *de restitutione spoliatorum*, "Ex conquestione" [X 2.13.10]; Extra *de divortiis*, "Porro" [X 4.19.3]; and this whole distinction is found at:Extra *de restitutione spoliatorum*, "Litteras" [X 2.13.13].

[6] RdeP: Extra *de divortiis*, "Significasti" [X 4.19.4].

[7] RdeP: Extra *de restitutione spoliatorum*, "Litteras" (circa finem) [X 2.13.13].

[8] RdeP: as is argued: Extra *de officio delegati*, "Causam matrimonii" [X 1.29.16].

[9] RdeP: Extra *de restitutione spoliatorum*, "Ex transmissa" [X 2.13.8], "Litteras" (in fine) [X 2.13.13].

[10] RdeP: Extra *de officio delegati*, "Consultationibus" [X 1.29.10]; Extra *Qui filii sint legitimi*, "Causam" (2) [X 4.17.7].

[11] RdeP: 32 q. 1 "De Benedicto" [*Decretum* C. 32 q.1 c.5].

2.   In regard to the third case (the second last above), suppose that the Church, deceived by false witnesses or in another way, proclaims a divorce between a couple. Then the man becomes a priest. Afterwards it is discovered that the Church was deceived. Is the priest to be restored to his wife?

I believe that if he cannot be induced to continence the man ought to be restored to her because even a monk would be restored to her. He is bound to pay the debt to his wife when she asks, but must not ask because he solemnized a vow as far as he himself was concerned.[12]

3.   What if a woman acted as possessor and she lost the case? Can she afterwards act as claimant?

You should say she can, but, if she acted as claimant and lost, she cannot afterwards act as possessor. If she began to act but did not carry it through and witnesses had not yet been called, nor had the case been fully presented, she can dismiss the petitory judgment and begin a possessory action.[13] And the law says that he who began to bring a claim does not seem to renounce possession and he can attack the decision concerning possession when the proceeding for restitution has been dismissed.[14]

4.   In sum, note that if an accused confessed in judgment what the plaintiff charged, his confession must stand unless through that confession there occurred prejudice to the marriage in question, or even to another marriage, for then collusion is feared.[15] If, indeed, one questioned in law denies what is charged, the one making the charge ought to offer proof and if he offers no proof he loses.[16]

Again, it must not be overlooked that one must be restored to everything he proved himself despoiled of, and to enjoy peaceful possession and full security.[17] But if a woman says she fears her husband will harm her in her person or possessions, as long as she shows probable cause why she suspects him, it pertains to the office of a judge to order that care be taken for her that the husband will treat her in bed and board and in everything as a husband ought to treat his wife, and that he not harm her in her person or possessions, or in any way dishonour her except in the case of appropriate marital correction. The husband ought to

<hr/>

[12] RdeP: see *Summa de paenitentia*, De votis, § "Item alter coniugum" et § "Item, quid si maritus" where these matters are sufficiently treated [Raymond of Penyafort, *Summa de paenitentia* 1.8.12 and 15 (ed. Ochoa and Díez, col. 357, 358)].

[13] RdeP: Extra *de causa possessionis et proprietatis*, "Pastoralis" [X 2.12.5].

[14] RdeP: ff. *de acquirenda possessione*, Lex "Naturaliter, § Nihil commune" [*Dig.* 41.2.12, 1].

[15] RdeP: Extra *de clandestina desponsatione*, "Quod nobis" [X 4.3.2]; Extra *de eo qui cognovit consanguineam uxoris suae*, "Super eo" [X 4.13.5].

[16] RdeP: Extra *de causa possessionis et proprietatis*, "Cum Ecclesia" [X 2.12.3]; Extra *de iureiurando*, c. ult. [X 2.24.36].

[17] RdeP: 3 q. 1 "Redintegranda" [*Decretum* C 3 q.1 c.3].

offer his guarantee under oath.[18] But if the woman does not trust the husband's oath because he might have little fear of the oath, he ought to offer a guarantee that he fears more, namely a pledged or secured guarantee under threat of punishment.[19]

[18] RdeP: 32 q. 1 "De Benedicto" [*Decretum* C. 32 q.1 c.5].

[19] RdeP: Arg. Extra *ut lite non contestata*, "Quoniam frequenter § ult." [X 2.6.5]; 23 q. 5 "Prodest" [*Decretum* C. 23 q.5 c.4]; q. 4 "Ea vindicta" [*Decretum* C. 23 q.4 c.51].

# Title XX
## Divorce on account of Consanguinity or Another Perpetual Impediment

How to act to preserve a marriage has been spoken of above, but because many unions are dissolved, how marriage is dissolved must be examined next. Because accusation must precede divorce, we must first examine who can bring an accusation against a marriage and testify against it, and how the accusation must be made.

1.  For this it should be known that anyone who is not forbidden can bring an accusation against a marriage to secure a complete divorce.

Generally, all strangers are prohibited as long as there are some of the blood relatives of the spouses, who wish and are able to bring an accusation against a marriage. However, in the absence of blood relatives older and more truthful neighbours, to whom the relationship is known, are admitted.

And this is a special case that blood relatives are admitted to bring an accusation against a marriage, such as a father, mother, brother, sister, paternal uncle, maternal uncle, paternal aunt, maternal aunt, and all their offspring.[1] The reason is because each labours to know his own genealogy both through witnesses and charters as well as through the accounts of elders. Nevertheless, in many places today this is not observed since strangers are heard in accusations even when blood relations exist who could be heard. Again, both a husband and wife are able to bring an accusation in a marriage, but both spouses as well as strangers at one time were prohibited from making an accusation in reference to length of time, namely if the spouses remained together without question for twenty or eighteen years. Laws were published in the matter and many comments made on them.

All of them were expressly revoked by the constitution of the General Council:[2] "Therefore, since the prohibition of conjugal union is now restricted up to the fourth degree, we wish it to be perpetual, notwithstanding constitutions on the matter once issued by others or by ourselves, so that if one should presume to be united against this prohibition length of years is not a defence since length of time does not diminish sin but increases it. The longer they hold the soul bound, the graver the crimes."

---

[1] RdeP: 35 q. 6 c. 1 et 2 [*Decretum* C. 35 q.6 c.1-2]; Extra *qui matrimonium accusare possunt*, "Videtur nobis" [X 4.18.3].

[2] RdeP: Extra *de consanguinitate et affinitate*, "Non debet § Prohibitio" [X 4.14.8].

2.    Suppose someone remained silent at the time of the marriage contract and afterwards wishes to bring an accusation against the marriage. Can he?

For this matter the distinction in the decretal is enough:[3] "If, indeed, after a marriage is contracted an accuser appears, since he did not speak out in public when the bans were published by custom in the churches, we can well ask whether his accusation should be admitted. On this we are led to make the following distinction: if at the time of the aforesaid announcement he who attacks the marriage was outside the diocese, or the announcement could not reach him for some other reason, so that, for example, labouring under a fever from serious illness his sanity deserted him, or he was of such tender years that his age was not up to understanding such matters, or if he was impeded by some other lawful cause, his accusation ought to be heard. Otherwise, when it is reasonably presumed that while living in the same diocese he was in no way ignorant of the public announcement, undoubtedly he is to be rejected as suspect unless he has sworn that he learned afterwards about what he objected to, and did not approach the matter out of malice, then even if he learned from those who were silent at the time of the announcement, access to making an accusation ought not be closed to them. The reason is because, although this type of fault based on such silence would bar one from making an accusation, this fault cannot be removed since he is not at fault."

From what has been said about accusation, it is clear who can bear witness against a marriage and who cannot, since all who are allowed to accuse are allowed to bear witness as long as they are persons with legal standing to testify. Otherwise, those who are prohibited from accusing are prohibited from bearing witness.

3.    In sum, note that if an accusation is made against the bond of marriage, that is, because the marriage is said to be null on account of consanguinity or another perpetual impediment, it is possible to proceed without initiating a trial to the reception of witnesses and even to a definitive judgment against one who fails to appear. If, however, the accusation of adultery is made for separation from bed, it is otherwise.[4]

Again, although a father and mother are suitable witnesses for their son or daughter where it is a question of the marriage bond, that is, whether there is between the ones in question such consanguinity as to impede marriage or not, yet, if it is about the contract itself,[5] that is, the question is aired whether marriage was contracted between them, they are to be rejected as suspect where the one whose son or daughter is claimed to be joined is superior in riches, nobility, power, or honour. This is because parents are seen to love the honour and advancement of their children.[6]

---

[3] RdeP: Extra *qui matrimonium accusare possunt*, "Cum in tua" and below [X 4.18.6].

[4] RdeP: Extra *ut lite non contestata*, c. 1 [X 2.6.1], et c. "Quoniam frequenter § Porro" [X 2.6.5].

[5] RdeP: Extra *qui matrimonium accusare possunt*, "Videtur nobis" [X 4.18.3].

[6] RdeP: Extra *de testibus*, "Super eo quod" [X 2.20.22].

Again, in a marriage case the same person can be accuser and witness.[7]

[7] RdeP: arg. 35 q. 6 "Episcopus in synodo" [*Decretum* C. 35 q.6 c.7], "De parentela" [*Decretum* C. 35 q.6 c.8]; Extra *de testibus cogendis*, "Praeterea" [X 2.21.7].

# Title XXI
## How an Accusation Is to Be Made against a Marriage

After we have treated of those who can bring an accusation against a marriage and who cannot, next we must see how an accusation ought to be made. For this note that in regard to marriage the term accusation is used improperly because no writing is done, but it is called denunciation, which is done on account of the sin in which they persist. However, denunciation is made sometimes in writing, sometimes without writing; but it is better and safer that it be done in writing.[1]

1. This is a form of accusation or denunciation: "I, so-and-so, say or denounce to you lord bishop that the marriage of Peter and Mary cannot stand because they are consanguine relations in such a degree," or if there is another reason for divorce, I ought to put it in a written complaint.

Further, in consanguinity or affinity [cases] another written complaint is customarily made and shown to the opposed party that he might know who is accused, which party wishes to bring proof, and in which the degrees of consanguinity are noted along with the proper names of the designated persons. After the written complaint is offered an oath is received from the parties to tell the truth and examination and proof are done in order.

2. Suppose that two brothers or two [male] consanguine relations have two sisters or two consanguine relations as wives. A judgment of divorce between one and his wife is rendered by the Church because of consanguinity. The question arises whether the other, on account of this, can be separated from his wife, or how he ought to conduct himself with her.

To this say that in no way can he be separated on account of this, because something done between some does not prejudice others.[2]

However, as far as carnal union is concerned I make a distinction: either he knows that consanguinity or another perpetual impediment exists between himself and his wife, or he believes it. In the first case he should neither demand nor pay [the debt]. In the second, if he believes for a probable reason, he should pay, but not ask. However, if he believes for a slight or inconsiderable reason, he should pay, and if he can, lay aside his erroneous conscience and afterwards demand.[3]

---

[1] RdeP: arg. Extra *de restitutione spoliatorum*, "Litteras" [X 2.13.13]; Extra *qui matrimonium accusare possunt*, "A nobis" [X 4.18.2].

[2] RdeP: Extra *de fide instrumentorum*, "Inter dilectos" [X 2.22.6].

[3] RdeP: Extra *de sententia excommunicationis*, "Inquisitioni" [X 5.39.44].

3.   In sum, it must not be overlooked that in a marriage already contracted there is place for accusation, but not in the contracting, because accusation has no place since there is nothing that can be accused. But consanguinity can be denounced or another impediment for which marriage is prohibited.[4]

Again, before a marriage or an engagement is contracted denunciation alone without proof is enough, if no oath was added. Otherwise, it is necessary to establish public report at least.[5]

---

[4] RdeP: Extra *de desponsatione impuberum*, "Ad dissolvendum" [X 4.2.13].

[5] RdeP: Extra *de sponsalibus*, "Praeterea de muliere" [X 4.1.12]; Extra *de consanguinitate et affinitate*, "Super eo quod" [X 4.14.2].

# Title XXII
## Divorce on account of Fornication

In the previous title it has been sufficiently shown who are permitted to bring an accusation against marriage and how it is to be done when full divorce is sought. In the following we must look a who is permitted to bring accusation that is made on account of fornication when it is a question of separation from bed and the relaxation of mutual service. Such accusation is more properly called accusation than the one spoken of in the preceding title, since this is done on account of the crime of adultery and in writing. Again, although both according to the canons and according to the laws anyone of good reputation is admitted to the accusation of adultery when it is a question of the infliction of legal or canonical penalty, yet when it is a question of the separation from bed no one is admitted to the accusation of marriage that is made on account of the commission of adultery except the husband and wife. We intend to treat of this in the present title.

Therefore, we must examine how such an accusation ought to be made; when the husband is prohibited from the accusation of his adulterous wife; what the effect of the accusation is if he proves his case.

1.  In regard to the first point you should hold that a husband, wishing to accuse his wife of adultery before a secular judge for legal penalty, ought to write, that is, to prepare a bill of accusation and bind himself to a penalty similar in kind. But if he wishes to accuse her before an ecclesiastical judge for separation from bed, he is bound to give her a bill of accusation, but ought not bind himself to a penalty similar in kind since, whether he proves his case or not, he would have what he wishes, that is, he would be deprived of his wife's embraces.[1]

Note that in this accusation, as in other matrimonial cases, the husband can accuse and she respond through a representative although it would be more securely done in the presence of the principal persons.[2]

The form of such a bill of accusation ought to be: "In the year of our Lord Jesus Christ MCCXXXV, presiding lord," etc.

2.  Next we must see when a husband can accuse his wife of adultery and when not, or vice versa the wife her husband, because in this case they are not judged as unequals.[3]

---

[1] RdeP: Extra *de procuratoribus*, "Tuae fraternitatis" [X 1.38.5].

[2] RdeP: as is said in the same decretal: "Tuae fraternitatis" [X 1.38.5].

[3] RdeP: 32 q. 1 "Si quis uxorem" [*Decretum* C. 32 q.1 c.4], and q. 5 "Praecepit Dominus" [Gra-

Indeed, it is generally true that a husband can accuse and dismiss his wife on account of fornication, and vice versa, the Lord saying in the gospel, "Everyone who dismisses his wife, except for reason of fornication, makes her commit adultery, and he who marries the dismissed wife commits adultery" (cf. Matt. 5.32). This reason is extended to the suspicion of fornication, by which I mean where the suspicion is so strong that after it is proven it would rightly seem that the fornication itself is proven, for example, if it was proven that they were alone together, naked, lying in the same bed, in a secret place and time suited for this.[4]

Again, I believe it is extended to the sodomitic crime so that a wife is able to dismiss her husband for it, and vice versa.[5] Again, it is also to be understood of spiritual fornication, for example, if the husband or wife should fall into heresy, Judaism, or the error of paganism.[6] But there is a difference here, because a man can dismiss his wife and the wife her husband on account of carnal fornication once committed. However, he cannot on account of spiritual fornication, if she wishes to correct herself.[7]

3.    Nevertheless, there are some cases in which an adulterous wife cannot be accused by her husband.

First, if he himself was convicted of fornicating.[8]

Second, if he offered her in prostitution.[9]

Third is when she believed her husband to be dead and she married another because when the husband returns he is bound to take her back notwithstanding such adultery unless she remained knowingly with the second husband after the first came back.[10]

The fourth is if she was known secretly by someone whom she believed to be her own husband.[11]

The fifth is if she was oppressed by force.[12] However, I understand this of absolute force, for if by fear, the order of parents, the insistence of blood relatives, or another similar cause she fornicates with him, even contracting with him in fact,

---

tian C. 32 q.5 c.19], "Christiana" [*Decretum* C. 32 q.5 c. 23].

[4] RdeP: 32 q. 1 "Dixit Dominus in Evangelio," the verse: "Therefore, wherever there is fornication or the suspicion of fornication the wife is freely dismissed." [*Decretum* C. 32 q.1 c.2]; Extra *de praesumptionibus*, "Litteris tuae fraternitatis" [X 2.23.12].

[5] RdeP: 32 q. 7 "Omnes causationes" [*Decretum* C. 32 q.7 c.7], "Adulterii malum" [*Decretum* C. 32 q.7 c.11].

[6] RdeP: 28 q. 1 "Idololatria " [*Decretum* C. 28 q.1 c.5]; Extra *de divortiis*, "Quaesivit" [X 4.19.2], "De illa" [X 4.19.6], "Quanto" [X 4.19.7].

[7] RdeP: Extra *de divortiis*, "De illa" [X 4.19.6].

[8] RdeP: 32 q. 6, per totum [*Decretum* C. 32 q.6]; Extra *de divortiis*, "Significasti" [X 4.19.4].

[9] RdeP: Extra *de eo qui cognovit consanguineam uxoris suae*, "Discretionem" [X 4.13.6].

[10] RdeP: 34 q. 2 "Cum per bellicam" [*Decretum* C. 34 q.2 c.1], "Si virgo" [*Decretum* C. 34 q.2 c.5].

[11] RdeP: as the argument: 34 q. 2 "In lectum mariti" [*Decretum* 34 q.2 c.6].

[12] RdeP: 32 q. 5 "Proposito" [*Decretum* C. 32 q.5 c.4].

she is not excused.[13]

The sixth is when he reconciled with her after the commission of adultery or he keeps her in marital union while she publicly commits adultery.[14]

The seventh (although it rarely happens) is that, if an unbeliever dismisses an unbelieving wife, providing himself with a bill of divorce, and she marries another according to her rite, if he [her first husband] was converted to the faith and she too, he is bound to take her back. This, notwithstanding that she was known by another with whom she joined, unless she otherwise fornicated.[15]

4. If the husband proves his case or the woman confesses, unless the woman comes back at him with one of the aforementioned seven cases, the effect of this accusation is that he is absolved from cohabiting with her and from the service he is bound to, and he can assume the habit of religious life against her wishes.[16] He can live in the world without her, yet he is bound to be continent as along as she lives.

5. Suppose that a judgment of divorce was rendered for the separation from bed because of the adultery of the wife and afterwards the husband commits adultery. The question arises whether the woman can demand him back, regardless of the judgment.

Solution: some say she cannot and I believe it is true in terms of legal rigor.[17] But the judge, in virtue of his office, ought to force him to return to his wife.[18]

Suppose the husband wishes to reconcile her to himself after the judgment and she does not want it. Must she be forced or does she sin if she does not return?

It seems to me that if the husband is innocent because he did not sin by adultery, he can seek her reconciliation to him even if she is unwilling, regardless of the judgment, because what was introduced in my favour should not be twisted into my harm.[19]

Suppose the husband committed adultery in secret, the wife openly. Can the husband accuse her and dismiss her through a judgment without sinning?

---

[13] RdeP: 32 q. 7 "Omnes causationes" [Decretum C. 32 q.7 c.7].

[14] RdeP: 32 q. 1, c. 1, 2, et 3 [Decretum C. 32 q.1 c.1-3]; C. ad legem Iuliam de adulteriis, "Crimen adulterii" [Code 9.9.11].

[15] RdeP: Extra de divortiis, "Gaudemus § ult." [X 4.19.8].

[16] RdeP: 27 q. 2 "Agathosa" [Decretum C. 27 q.2 c.21].

[17] RdeP: arg. 6 q. 4: "What was well defined once ought not be retracted by any repetition." [Decretum C. 6 q.4 c.6].

[18] RdeP: arg. Extra de iureiurando "Tua nos" [X 2.24.24]; Extra de divortiis, "Ex litteris" [X 4.19.5]; and the Apostle to the Corinthians: "To those who are married not I but the Lord orders that the wife not depart from her husband and that if she departs she remain unmarried or be reconciled with her husband. And the husband should not dismiss his wife" (1 Cor. 7.10-11).

[19] RdeP: C. de legibus, "Quod favore" [Code 1.14.6].

I believe not because the wife does not lose the right, but proof.[20] But if the husband did penance and the wife refused to do penance after being warned but persevered in adultery, I believe that he could accuse her without sin and dismiss her through a judgment.[21]

But can an adulterous wife after penance bar her husband from accusation, or vice versa the husband his wife?

It seems so because as Gregory says, "he ought not be despised in what he was, because he already begins to be what he was not."[22] Nonetheless, I believe the contrary because penance does not take away the right of accusing or of opposing or of responding in the judicial or contentious forum.[23] It must be shown whether he was not criminal beforehand.[24]

[20] RdeP: arg. 32 q. 6, per totum [Decretum C. 32 q.6].

[21] RdeP: 32 q. 1 c. 1, 2, 3, et 4 [Decretum C. 32 q.1 c.1-4].

[22] RdeP: dist. 50 "Ferrum" [Decretum D. 50 c.18].

[23] RdeP: dist. 25 "Primum" [Decretum D. 25 c.6]; 33 q. 2 "Admonere" [Decretum C. 33 q.2 c.8]; 6 q. 1 "Qui crimen intendit" [Gratian C. 6 q.1 c.6].

[24] RdeP: Extra de testibus, "Testimonium" [X 2.20.54].

# Title XXIII
## The Number of Witnesses Both in Matrimony as well as in Other Cases

1. Finally, we must examine how many witnesses suffice in a matrimonial case. Generally, it is true that two witnesses are enough. As a general rule, this many suffice in every case as Truth himself testifies in the gospel (cf. John 8.17).[1]

2. This rule fails in some cases in which a specified number is stated.[2]

One case is if by chance a cleric of the Roman Church is accused, more witnesses than two would be required.[3] Yet some understand this in a particular case, for otherwise two good witnesses would be enough even in this case.[4]

Another case is where one of ill fame must purge himself of a crime.[5]

Again, in testaments seven are required,[6] in codicils and last wills, five.[7] But it seems these laws should not hold because of certain decretals where it is said expressly that even in testaments two or three witnesses are enough, because of the decretals.[8] Or these decretals are to be restricted to pious cases such as if in the will or codicils something were bequeathed to poor churches or other godly places, it would have force for them even with two or three witnesses.

Again, although some cases require more than two witnesses, there is none in which one is enough, however meritorious he may be.[9] Yet, there is a case in which one witness would be enough.[10]

---

[1] RdeP: and Extra *de testibus*, "In omni negotio" [X 2.20.4]; 2 q. 4 § 1 [*Decretum* C. 2 q.4 d.p.c.1].

[2] RdeP: 4 q. 3 "Ubi numerus" [*Decretum* C. 4 q.3 d.p.c.2, § 26].

[3] RdeP: 2 q. 4 "Praesul" [*Decretum* C. 2 q.4 c.2], "Nullam" [*Decretum* C. 2 q.4 c.3].

[4] RdeP: 2 q. 4 § ult. [*Decretum* C. 2 q.4 d.p.c.3].

[5] RdeP: see *Summa de paenitentia*, in titulo De purgationibus, § "Circa processum, versu Est autem digna satisfactio" [Raymond of Penyafort, *Summa de paenitentia* 3.31.5 (ed. Ochoa and Díez, col. 717)].

[6] RdeP: C. *de testamentis*, "Hac consultissima" [*Code* 6.23.21].

[7] RdeP: C. *de codicillis*, Lex ult. (in fine) [*Code* 6.36.8].

[8] RdeP: Extra *de testamentis*, "Cum esses" and "Relatum" [X 3.26.10-11].

[9] RdeP: Extra *de testibus*, "Licet universis" [X 2.20.23], "Cum a nobis" [X 2.20.28]; 4 q. 3 "Iurisiurandi" [*Decretum* C. 4 q.3 d.p.c.2, § 37].

[10] RdeP: see *Summa de paenitentia*, in titulo De sacramentis, § "Post praedicta, versu Unus quando dubitatur" [Raymond of Penyafort, *Summa de paenitentia* 3.24.8 (ed. Ochoa and Díez, col. 664)]. [The case in question is when there is a doubt about whether a church was initially consecrated and there is an absence of written proofs, "nor does even one witness appear who saw [the consecration] or heard about it."]

# Title XXIV
## Who are Legitimate Children and Who Are Not

Marriage was treated above, but since marriages are contracted because of children, we should next deal with children themselves, showing which children are legitimate and which are not, how the illegitimate are legitimated, and what the advantage of being legitimate is.

1.  A legitimate child is one born of a legitimate marriage, or of one deemed legitimate in the eyes of the Church, although in truth it was no marriage.[1]

I believe this is true when both were united in good faith believing themselves legitimately joined or as long as one of them believes it. If a woman in good faith marries someone who is married believing him to be single and has children from him, they are judged to be legitimate and succeed to both parents.[2] If one should presume to enter into a clandestine or prohibited marriage in a forbidden degree, even if unknowingly, the offspring of such a union is to be considered utterly illegitimate. The ignorance of the parents offers no support, since by contracting in such a way they seem not to be devoid of knowledge or at least they seem to be affecting ignorance. In like manner, offspring is to be considered illegitimate if both parents, knowing the legitimate impediment, presume to contract marriage even in the eyes of the Church, contrary to all prohibition.[3]

2.  Again, note the status of children is four-fold: some are natural and legitimate such as those born of wives; others are only natural such as the children of concubines, such as are those born of a single man and a single woman, who could be a wife; others are legitimate alone, such as those adopted; others, who are neither legitimate nor natural, are called spurious, such as those who are born of adultery or incest.

3.  How the illegitimate are made legitimate follows. The first way is by a subsequent marriage, since if one has natural children from some woman and afterwards marries her, the children already born are legitimated. But if he has spurious

---

[1] RdeP: Extra *qui filii sint legitimi*, "Cum inter Ioannem" [X 4.17.2], "Gaudemus" [X 4.17.15].

[2] RdeP: Extra *qui filii sint legitimi*, "Ex tenore" [X 4.17.14].

[3] RdeP: 35 q. 3 "Coniunctiones" [*Decretum* C. 35 q.3 c.2]; Extra *qui filii sint legitimi*, "Referente" [X 4.17.10]; and is expressed at: Extra *de clandestina desponsatione*, "Cum inhibitio, § Si quis vero" [X 4.3.3].

children from her, they are not made legitimate.[4]

The second way is by special indulgence of the lord pope.[5]

These two are found to be according to the canons. Some others follow according to the civil laws. One is if the father offers the child to the court of the emperor and he becomes a courtier, he becomes legitimate whether the father has legitimate children or not.[6]

Again, if a deceased father names him in a testament as a legitimate heir and he [the child] afterwards offers the testament to the prince wishing to be made legitimate, he would receive the right of the legitimate.

The third way is if, after the father dies without any legitimate child, the natural child offers himself.[7]

The fourth way according to the laws is if the father in a public instrument or with the written subscription of three witnesses, names him as his child and does not add [he was] natural, he becomes legitimate.[8]

4.    It benefits children to be legitimate because they succeed to all the goods of their parents.[9] And they are deemed suited to all legitimate acts. Natural children can succeed only to two twelfths, that is, to a sixth of the inheritance of the father, if the father himself has children, or parents, or a wife. But if the deceased has no children, parents, or wife, the father in a testament can bestow his whole inheritance on his natural children among the living.[10]

Spurious children and those who are from censured intercourse are excluded entirely from any benefit. Nevertheless, it will be one of the bishop's concerns that both parents, according to their abilities, supply for the needs of such children.[11]

---

[4] RdeP: as is stated expressly at: Extra *qui filii sint legitimi*, "Conquestus" [X 4.17.1], "Tanta est vis" [X 4.17.6]; Inst. *de nuptiis*, § ult. [*Inst.* 1.10,13].

[5] RdeP: Extra *qui filii sint legitimi*, "Per venerabilem" [X 4.17.13].

[6] RdeP: Auth. *quibus modis naturales efficiuntur legitimi*, § "Si quis igitur," collat. 7 (*Novels* 89.2, 1).

[7] RdeP: You have all these methods in Auth. *quibus modis naturales efficiantur sui*, § 1 et § "Si quis igitur," collat. 7 (*Novels* 89.2, 1).

[8] RdeP: Auth. *ut liceat matri et aviae*, "Ad hoc," collat. 8 (*Novels* 117.2).

[9] RdeP: Auth. *quibus modis naturales efficiantur sui*, § "Et quoniam" (*Novels* 89.3); C. *de suis et legitimis heredibus*, per totum [*Code* 6.55] and in the previously alleged decretals.

[10] RdeP: C. *de naturalibus liberis*, Auth. *Licet patri* [*Code* 5.27.8, i.e., *Novels* 89.12 and 15].

[11] RdeP: Extra *de eo qui duxit in matrimonium quam polluit per adulterium*, "Cum habent" (in fine) [X 4.7.5].

# Title XXV
## The Dowry and Gifts in View of Marriage

Since it is in the public interest that women have their dowries secure so that they might be able to marry again, after the treatment of marriage we must discuss the dowry, which is an accessory to marriage.[1]

Judgment regarding the dowry pertains to an ecclesiastical judge, either the ordinary or his delegate. When a matrimonial case is initiated, the case of the dowry as an accessory to it is understood to be initiated.[2] Therefore, since the judge is familiar with the marriage, he ought likewise to judge of the dowry. This is observed in the city of Bologna (which has primacy and mastery in both canon and secular law) out of accepted custom – from the beginning of the legal suit or at least before a judgment is pronounced, the husband offers his wife a pledged or sworn security for the restoration of the dowry immediately or at an appropriate time if a judgment of divorce should be promulgated. Otherwise the judges never proceed with the case.

So we must examine: what a dowry is; the species of dowry; what *paraferna* is; what a gift for marriage is; in what cases a husband profits from the dowry; in what case he is bound to return the dowry, to whom, and when.

1.  A dowry is a certain kind of gift made on the part of the woman to the man for the burden of marriage that he bears. It is the nature of a dowry to last for the duration of a marriage, but when it dissolves the dowry dissolves because without it the dowry cannot be. The dowry itself is a sort of proper patrimony of the woman.[3]

2.  There are two species of dowry: one is profective,[4] the other adventive.[5] Profective dowry is what is given by a father for his daughter, or by a grandfather for his granddaughter, whether from their goods, or another gives on their command.[6] Adventive dowry is what the woman herself gives for herself or someone else other than the father or grandfather gives, whether brother, uncle, or anyone else.

---

[1] RdeP: ff. *de iure dotum*, 1, 2, et 3 [*Dig.* 23.3.2-3].

[2] RdeP: Extra *de donationibus inter virum et uxorem et dote post divortium restituenda*, c. 1, 2, 3 [X 4.20.1-3]; Extra *de coniugio servorum*, "Proposuit" [X 4.9.2].

[3] RdeP: ff. *de minoribus*, "Denique § Utrum" [*Dig.* 4.4.3, 4].

[4] Text: *profecticia*

[5] Text: *adventicia*

[6] RdeP: ff. *de iure dotium*, "Profecticia" [*Dig.* 23.3.5].

Again, one dowry given is appraised in value, the other not appraised in value. If what is appraised is given, both the gain and the loss belong to the husband, just as with the purchase of property. If what is not appraised is given, its loss and gain belong to the woman,[7] with the exception of the fruits which belong to the husband on account of the burdens of marriage he bears because he has to support his wife and children.[8]

3.  We saw what dowry is; let us see what *paraferna* is, and its etymology. *Paraferna* is what the woman has after or aside from the dowry, from whatever source. It is from παρα, which means beside, and φερνα, which means dowry; so *paraferna*, that is "beside the dowry". However, *paraferna* has a privilege on the model of dowry. Just as a woman has all the goods of her husband tacitly obligated for the dowry, so too for things given to her husband as *paraferna*.[9]

4.  A gift on account of marriage is what the male spouse gives to the female.[10] It is characteristic of such a gift, however, that if the husband entered into an agreement to profit from part of the dowry if his wife should predecease him, the woman ought to profit only from the gift given on account of the marriage if her husband should predecease her.[11]

5.  The husband profits from the dowry both by contract and by law. By contract if he entered into an agreement to gain the whole dowry or part of it.[12] By law the husband receives the dowry if the woman commits adultery, for after a divorce on account of the woman's adultery, the woman loses the dowry.[13] Likewise, after the intestate death of the woman without children and near relatives, the husband succeeds to the wife and receives the dowry, and vice versa.[14]

In cases other than the aforesaid, after the dissolution of the marriage the dowry reverts to the woman and the gift on account of marriage to the husband, unless it should be otherwise by approved custom.[15]

6.  Next we see to whom the dowry must be restored. And certainly the dowry coming from the father is to be returned to the father on the death of his daughter

---

[7] RdeP: ff. *de iure dotium*, "Plerumque" [*Dig.* 23.3.10].

[8] RdeP: ff. *de iure dotis*, "Plerumque" [*Dig.* 23.3.10], "Dotis fructus" [*Dig.* 23.3.7].

[9] RdeP: C. *de pactis conventis*, Lex ult. [*Code* 5.14.11].

[10] RdeP: Extra eodem, "Nuper" (in fine) [X 4.20.6].

[11] RdeP: Extra eodem, "Donatio § Sane" [X 4.20.8]; C. *de pactis conventis*, "Ex morte" [*Code* 5.14.19].

[12] RdeP: C. *de pactis conventis*, "Ex morte" [*Code* 5.14.19]; in Auth. ibi posita [*Code* 5.14.9].

[13] RdeP: as is said expressly in: Extra eodem, "Plerumque" [X 4.20.4], et in Auth., *ut liceat matri et aviae*, § "Quia vero" collat. 8 (*Novels* 117.8).

[14] RdeP: C. *unde vir et uxor*, Lex 1 [*Code* 6.18.1].

[15] RdeP: Extra eodem, "Mulieres" [X 4.20.1], "Donatio § Sane" [X 4.20. 8]; ff. *soluto matrimonio*, Lex paenult., § "Mulier" [*Dig.* 24.3.66, 4].

during the marriage.[16] If, however, a divorce occurs while the daughter and father are living, the dowry is to be returned to the father and the daughter.[17] But if the dowry is adventive, it must be returned to the woman.[18]

However, my claim, "dowry coming from the father is to be returned to the father" some doctors of law understand to obtain if the woman dies without children. Otherwise, it remains with the children.[19] Others say the contrary, but the first opinion is stronger.

Finally, we must see when the dowry should be restored. It should be held that if the dowry consists in possessions, that is, in immoveable things such as properties or houses, it must be returned immediately on the dissolution of the marriage. If they are moveable things such as money, clothing, or animals, they are to be returned within a year.[20]

7.   In sum, it must be noted that a husband in returning the dowry is only condemned to the extent he is able to return it without leaving himself in need, as is said in the same law.[21] This privilege passes to the children of the same marriage.[22]

Further, it should be noted that the husband, on returning the dowry can hold back necessary and useful expenses undertaken in matters of the dowry, for example, because he renovated the house.[23] Yet he loses [what was expended on] pleasures.[24]

---

[16] RdeP: C. *soluto matrimonio,* "Dos a patre" [*Code* 5.18.4].

[17] RdeP: ff. *soluto matrimonio,* Lex 1 et Lex "Post" [*Dig.* 24.3.1 and 40].

[18] RdeP: ff. *soluto matrimonio,* "Quotiens" § 1 [*Dig.* 24.3.29, 1].

[19] RdeP: ff. *soluto matrimonio,* Lex "Post dotem" [*Dig.* 24.3.40].

[20] RdeP: this is all said: C. *de rei uxoriae actione,* Lex 1, § "Cum autem" [*Code* 5.13.1, 7].

[21] RdeP: [*Code* 5.13.1, 7]; ff. *de regulis iuris,* Lex "In condemnatione" [*Dig.* 50.17.173]; et *de re iudicata,* Lex "Sunt qui" [*Dig.* 42.1.16], with the following law [*Dig.* 42.1.17].

[22] RdeP: ff. *soluto matrimonio,* "Maritum" [*Dig.* 24.3.12].

[23] RdeP: ff. *de impensis in rebus dotalibus factis,* Lex 1 [*Dig.* 25.1.1].

[24] RdeP: as is said there [*Dig.* 25.1.1].

# Conclusion

Although much more would have to be said about the dowry as well as about other points to have a full knowledge of marriage issues, nonetheless, for the sake of brevity the foregoing should suffice.

Asking for the indulgence of the reader for the imperfection of the work, let him correct and improve what he sees needs correction and addition, not in an envious but in a friendly spirit.

# Parallels between
## Raymond of Penyafort, *Summa on Marriage*
## and Thomas Aquinas

| Raymond of Penyafort *Summa on Marriage* | Thomas Aquinas *In 4 Sent.* | Thomas Aquinas *Summa Theologiae,* Supplementum |
|---|---|---|
| 1 | D. 7.2.1-3 | 43.1-3 |
| 2.23 | D. 7.1.2 (1)-(4); D. 28.1.3 | 45.1-5 |
| | D. 28.1.1-2 | 46.1-2 |
| | D. 28.1.4; D. 30.1.3 | 48.1-2 |
| 4.2 | D. 36.1.1-4 | 52.4 ad 3 |
| 7 | D 42.1.1-3 | 56.1-5 |
| 8 | D. 42.2.1-3 | 57.1-3 |
| 9 | cf. D. 35, *expositio textus* | |
| 11.3 | D. 29.1.1-4 | 47.2 |
| 14 | D. 41.1.1 (4) | 55.4 |
| 16 | D. 34.1.2-3 | cf. 58.1-2 |
| 18 | D. 32.1.5 (4) | |
| 20 | D. 41.1.5 | 55.9-11 |
| 21 | D. 41.1.5 (2) | 55.10 |
| 22.3 | D. 35.1.1 | 62.1 |
| 24 | D. 41.3.3 | 68.1-3 |

# Index of Legal References

The following legal references are followed in brackets by the Title number and paragraph number where the references can be found in the translation, e.g. (2.4) refers to Title 2, paragraph 4. Where only one numeral appears it is a case of there being no paragraph numbers such as in Title 12, or the reference is made in an unnumbered introductory paragraph of a title.

## ROMAN LAW

*Authenticum (= Novels)*

22.6 (16.4)
89.2,1 (24.3)
89.3 (24.4)
117.2 (24.3)
117.8 (25.5)

*Code*

1.14.6 (22.5)
1.18.8 (3.1)
1.18.9 (3.1)
5.1.3 (1.1)
5.13.1, 7 (25.6)
5.14.11 (25.3)
5.14.19 (25.4)
5.18.4 (25.6)
5.27.8 (= *Novels* 89.12
    and 15) (24.4)
6.18.1 (25.5)
6.23.21 (23.2)
6.36.5 (2.7)
6.36.8 (23.2)

6.55 (24.4)
8.47.1 (8.4)
8.47.5 (8.3)
8.47.10 (8.4)
9.9.11 (22.3)

*Digest*

1.7.2 (8.2)
1.7.2, 1 (8.3)
1.7.15 (8.2)
1.7.15, 3 (8.3)
1.7.16 (8.3)
1.7.21 (8.3)
1.7.23 (8.5)
2.1.15 (3.1)
4.2.1 (11.2)
4.2.2 (11.2)
4.2.7 (11.3)
4.2.8 (11.3)
4.2.23 (11.3)
4.4.3, 4 (25.1)
18.1.41, 1 (3.1)

23.1.1 (1.1)
23.2.1 (2.1)
23.2.14 (8.6)
23.3.1-3 (25)
23.3.5 (25.2)
23.3.7 (25.3)
23.3.10 (25.2)
24.3.1 (25.6)
24.3.12 (25.7)
24.3.29, 1 (25.6)
24.3.40 (25.6)
24.3.66, 4 (25.5)
25.1.1 (25.7)
27.1.17 (1.5)
41.2.12, 1 (19.3)
42.1.16-17 (25.7)
50.17.173 (25.7)

*Institutes*

1.9, 1 (2.1)
1.10, 1-3 (8.6)
1.10, 13 (24.3)

## GRATIAN, *DECRETUM*

D. 25 c.6 (22.5)
D. 26 c.4 (10.2)
D. 27 c.3 (5.6)

D. 27 c.4 (5.6)
D. 27 c.6 (5.4)
D. 28 c.5 (12)

D. 32 c.3 (12)
D. 32 d.p.c.6. (7.7; 10.6)
D. 32 c.7 (12)

C. 35 q.5 c.6 (6.2)
C. 35 q.6 c.1 (20.1)
C. 35 q.6 c.2 (20.1)

C. 35 q.6 c.7 (20.3)
C. 35 q.6 c.8 (20.3)
C. 35 q.10 c.1 (15.4)

*De consec.*

D. 4 c.100 (7.7)

## COMPILATIONES

*Comp. II*
3.20. (10.1)

## DECRETALS (X)

1.6.29 (6.5)
1.7.2 (7.5)
1.21.5 (2.15)
1.29.5 (4.2)
1.29.16 (19.1)
1.29.19 (19.1)
1.38.4 (2.8)
1.38.5 (22.1)
1.40.1 (11.3)
1.40.4 (11.3)
1.40.5 (11.3)
1.40.6 (11.3)
2.6.1 (20.3)
2.6.5 (16.3; 19.4; 20.3)
2.9.4 (17.2)
2.10.1 (19.1)
2.12.3 (16.5; 19.4)
2.12.5 (19.3)
2.13.8 (19.1)
2.13.10 (19.1)
2.13.13 (19.1; 21)
2.16.2 (2.11)
2.19.4 (16.5)
2.10.4 (23.1)
2.20.22 (20.3)
2.20.23 (23.2)
2.20.28 (23.2)
2.20.47 (6.4)
2.20.54 (22.5)
2.21.7 (20.3)
2.22.6 (21.2)
2.23.11 (2.1)
2.23.12 (22.2)
2.24.18 (1.7)

2.24.24 (22.5)
2.24.25 (1.7)
2.24.36 (16.5; 19.4)
2.27.26 (2.8; 16.5)
3.3.1-3 (12)
3.26.10-11 (23.2)
3.31.4 (5.4)
3.31.8 (5.3)
3.31.9 (5.4)
3.31.11 (5.3)
3.31.13 (5.4)
3.31.14 (5.3)
3.31.15 (5.2)
3.31.22 (5.5)
3.32.2 (1.7; 13.2)
3.32.7 (1.7; 13.2)
3.42.3 (2.8)
3.43.1 (7.7)
3.43.3 (7.7)
4.1.1 (14.1)
4.1.2 (1.7)
4.1.3 (14.1)
4.1.4 (14.1; 14.2)
4.1.5 (1.1; 1.6; 1.7)
4.1.6 (11.1)
4.1.9 (1.1)
4.1.10 (1.6)
4.1.12 (1.1; 21.3)
4.1.13 (9.2)
4.1.14 (1.6; 11.1)
4.1.15 (11.3)
4.1.17 (1.6)
4.1.18 (9.2)
4.1.19 (13.4)

4.1.21 (11.4)
4.1.22 (1.7; 13.1)
4.1.23 (2.2; 2.7)
4.1.25 (2.2; 2.7)
4.1.26 (2.4)
4.1.29 (1.6)
4.1.31 (1.1; 1.7; 2.2)
4.1.32 (1.5)
4.2.2 (1.6)
4.2.3 (1.2; 1.5)
4.2.4 (1.2; 1.4; 14.1)
4.2.5 (1.2; 1.4; 1.6; 14.1)
4.2.6 (1.2; 1.5; 14.1; 16.5)
4.2.7 (1.6; 1.7)
4.2.8 (1.5; 1.6; 1.7)
4.2.9-11 (1.5)
4.2.12 (1.2; 1.3; 1.4; 1.5)
4.2.13 (21.3)
4.2.14 (1.3; 1.5)
4.3.2 (19.4)
4.3.3 (18.2; 24.1)
4.4.1 (1.1; 1.7; 13.1)
4.4.3 (13.2)
4.4.5 (1.1; 1.6; 2.2)
4.5.1 (4.3)
4.5.3 (4.3)
4.5.5 (1.3; 1.4; 4.3)
4.5.6 (4.3)
4.5.7 (4.3)
4.6.1-2 (12; 20.3)
4.6.3 (5.6)
4.6.4 (5.4)
4.6.6 (5.6)
4.6.7 (5.4)

# Subject Index

References are to pages.

monk, *see* orders, holy
Muslims, *see* religions, dissimilar
mutes and marriage 20

oaths 18; *see also* engagement
offspring, *see* children
orders, holy: entering 73; impediment of
    11, 56; taking of and marriage 35-37
orders, minor 56

pagans, *see* religions, dissimilar
parafema 87, 88
paralysis: dissolves engagement 17
paternity (spiritual relationship) and
    marriage 43, 45
peace, as reason for marriage 21
permanency of marriage 23
pledge, *see* engagement
pope 45; and legitimacy of children 86
priest, *see* orders, holy
procreation (in marriage), 64
prohibition of the church, impediment
    of 12, 70
promise, *see* engagement
prostitution, as cause for divorce 81
proxy marriage 22-23
public good, impediment of 11, 59-60

ratification of engagements or marriages
    before age of consent 15
religion, dissimilar, impediment of 11,
    51-53, 57, 82; and impotence 68
religions, other: their marriage laws 52
religious life 35; dissolves engagement
    17, 18; after marriage 23

restoration of spouse 71-2
riches, as reason for marriage 21
ring, engagement 13

sacraments 45-46
Saracens, *see* religions, dissimilar
separation because of adultery 71; be-
    cause of fornication 71; because of
    impediment 70; due to impotence 66;
    because of religious life 71; *see also* di-
    vorce
servitude, *see* condition, impediment of
sexual acts, unnatural 62
sin: mortal 25, 26; venal 25, 26
slavery and marriage 32-34
sodomy, as cause for divorce 81
spells, 64
spiritual relationship, impediment of 11,
    43-46
spouse: believed dead of 58, 81; disap-
    pearance 58, 81; return after absence,
    58, 81
subdeacon, see orders, holy

testicles: one only and marriage 22

violence, *see* coersion
virginity 67
vow: definition of 35; impediment of 11,
    35-38; and mental illness 35; mini-
    mum age 35, 36; simple 36, 37; sol-
    emn, 36-38; who can make 35; *see also*
    holy orders

wills and testaments 84
witnesses 73, 84